TO:

_____

FROM:

_____

DATE:

_____

STANDING FIRM

Christian art gifts®

Visit Christian Art Gifts, Inc. at www.christianartgifts.com

Standing Firm
Published by Christian Art Gifts, Inc.

Previously published as *God's Daily Promises for Leaders:
Daily Wisdom from God's Word*
First printing Tyndale House Publishers

Copyright © 2007 by Ron Beers. All rights reserved.

General Editors: Ron Beers and Amy Mason
Contributing Editor: Rebecca Beers
Contributing Writers: V. Gilbert Beers, Ronald A. Beers,
Brian R. Coffey, Jonathan Farrar, Jonathan Gray,
Shawn A. Harrison, Sandy Hall, Rhonda K. O'Brien,
Douglas J. Rumford
Edited by Michal Needham

Designed by Christian Art Gifts
Cover and interior images under license from Shutterstock.com

Scripture quotations are taken from the *Holy Bible*,
New Living Translation, copyright © 1996, 2004.
Used by permission of Tyndale House Publishers, Inc.,
Carol Stream, Illinois 60188. All rights reserved.

ISBN 978-1-77637-087-0 (Faux Leather)
ISBN 978-1-77637-147-1 (Paperback)

Printed in China

22 23 24 25 26 27 28 29 30 31 – 10 9 8 7 6 5 4 3 2 1

Introduction

Why did God make so many promises? Maybe it's because he wants to show you how much you can really trust him. Maybe he is so interested in you that he is trying to get your attention with each amazing promise he makes, wanting to show you just how much you have to look forward to as you travel through life.

This unique book presents more than 365 of these incredible promises, at least one for every day of the year. All these promises will come true—or have already come true. You simply have to decide whether you want to be part of them or not.

Imagine that every morning you could be inspired by a promise from God's Word and then live the rest of the day with either the expectation that God will fulfill that promise or the confidence that comes from a promise already fulfilled.

Standing Firm is designed to inspire you in just that way. Every page is dated, making the book easy to use. First, read the promise from God. Think about it. Let it soak in. Then read the short devotional note to help you look at your day differently because of God's promise.

Finally, read the question at the end to encourage and motivate you to trust that this promise was meant for you. Claim the promise as your own with the confidence that you can always trust God to keep his word. Our prayer is that you will be blessed and encouraged as you see and experience all that God has in store for you.

—The Editors

JANUARY

New Beginnings

*I am certain that God, who began
the good work within you, will continue
his work until it is finally finished
on the day when Christ Jesus returns.*

PHILIPPIANS 1:6

You harvest what you plant. Pumpkin seeds produce pumpkins. Sunflower seeds produce sunflowers. That is why you must ask the Lord to plant a clean heart in you so your life will produce clean thoughts, actions, and motives. If you have wrong desires and thoughts, it is evidence that some bad seeds were planted, and you need to do some weeding. Complete renewal cannot be accomplished yet because none of us will be entirely pure in this life. But developing purity of mind and heart is one of the most worthy goals you can pursue this year. What might you look like a year from now—inside and outside—if you accomplished that goal?

*What small seeds of godliness
can you plant today?*

Heavenly Goals

We can make our plans, but the LORD determines our steps.

PROVERBS 16:9

Goals give you direction. You may have many different goals for the different areas of your life, such as those New Year's resolutions you made. But you should make following God your primary goal.

You do not know what the year ahead will bring, but if the Lord determines your steps and you follow him, you can be sure that your life will have purpose in everything you do.

Determine never to stray from God, regardless of what life throws at you.

What would it take for you to follow God more closely each day?

Plan to Please God

*He renews my strength. He guides me along
right paths, bringing honor to his name.*

PSALM 23:3

*Even the Son of Man came not to be served
but to serve others and to give his life
as a ransom for many.*

MARK 10:45

Jesus sought to please his Father and give glory to him in everything he did. That plan shaped the way he lived each day and the way he served others in every interaction. As you begin each day of this new year, ask yourself two questions: *Will my plans for today please God? Will I be serving others today?*

If you can answer yes to these questions and then follow through with your actions, you will be on the right path—God's path for you. You will know how to spend your time, and you will become more like Jesus.

*How might asking yourself these two
questions each day shape your plans?*

Making Good Decisions

*Who are those who fear the LORD? He will
show them the path they should choose.*

PSALM 25:12

The Bible says that if you "fear the Lord," he will guide you through life. To fear the Lord means to respect him enough to obey him. When you obey him, you will follow him. And when you follow him, he will lead you to the places and opportunities where you can best serve him and other people.

If you want to make good decisions, first decide to obey God. Then you will know that you are going in the right direction with your other decisions.

*Have you decided to obey and follow God?
How does that affect the way
you make your decisions?*

Fresh Mercies Every Day

Great is his faithfulness; his mercies begin afresh each morning.

LAMENTATIONS 3:23

We all long for a new start, a clean slate, a chance to begin again. That's why many people get excited about New Year's resolutions. But every day is a new start when it comes to God's mercy. Every day you can ask forgiveness for your sins, and then he pours his mercy into you, cleaning you from the inside out. When that happens he doesn't see any sin in you. He doesn't see your failures; he sees you as his masterpiece.

By God's grace and love you are freed from the burden of sin and failure so that you can start fresh, both in your eyes and his. To lead others to experience true life change, you must embrace God's life-changing mercy.

Have you experienced God's mercy today?

Choose to Obey

Love the LORD your God and ...
keep his commands, decrees, and regulations
by walking in his ways. If you do this,
you will live and ... the LORD your God
will bless you.

DEUTERONOMY 30:16

Serving God with your whole life begins with little decisions to serve him. Commit yourself to making daily choices to serve God in the little things.

The more you do, the more you will want to obey all of God's commands. A life of obedience is a life committed to daily godly choices.

What small step of obedience
can you take today?

You Are Significant

What are mere mortals that you should think about them, human beings that you should care for them? Yet you made them only a little lower than God and crowned them with glory and honor.

PSALM 8:4-5

Deep within every human heart lies the desire for significance. We want our lives to count, to make a difference. Yet many of us carry deep feelings of insignificance. Everywhere we look, we see others who are more successful, more gifted, more this, more that.

The Bible promises that your life holds great potential. You are significant—not because of what you can accomplish in this life, but because of what God can accomplish through you that will last for eternity.

Do you focus on what you can't do or on what God can do through you?

Make Your Mark

*The more you grow like this, the more productive
and useful you will be in your knowledge
of our Lord Jesus Christ.*

2 PETER 1:8

Character is what you are, but it is also what you want to become. Ultimately, your character is the mark you make on the world around you. If you are striving for good character—better yet, for godly character—you are working toward moral excellence.

Think of all the areas in your life, such as career or hobbies, in which you've worked hard to develop excellence. Doesn't it also make sense to work hard at becoming morally excellent, mastering the things that really matter, such as integrity, kindness, love, and faithfulness?

You can do that by asking God to work through you as you relate to others.

———— • ————

*Your reputation, or what other people say
about you, is often a good measure
of your character. If you could hear others
talking about you, what might they be saying?*

Heavenly Plans

The LORD will work out his plans for my life.

PSALM 138:8

God's plan for your life is not like a written script that you must follow word for word; it's more like a journey with important destinations and appointments but with a great deal of freedom as to the pace and route of travel.

God's plan for you will always have a sense of mystery about it, but you can be certain that as you look for his leading, God will guide and direct you on your journey.

———————•———————

*Do you plan to follow God on
your journey through life?*

Doors of Opportunity

"I know the plans I have for you," says the LORD.
*"They are plans for good and not for disaster,
to give you a future and a hope."*

JEREMIAH 29:11

While it may seem like some things just happen, much of what determines the direction of your life is part of God's plan for you. If everything happens merely by chance, then either there is no God at all, or God is impersonal and detached from the human race. But the Bible says that God is not only real, he is also compassionate and deeply involved in his creation. In fact, he has an eternal plan for all of creation and for you.

While you may not understand how certain events in your life fit into God's perfect plan, you can be confident that God is watching over you and guiding you in a specific direction. He opens doors of opportunity, but you must walk through them. Will you follow where he leads?

*How can you recognize the doors of
opportunity God opens for you today?*

Don't Be Overwhelmed

Don't be afraid, for I am with you.
Don't be discouraged, for I am your God.
I will strengthen you and help you.
I will hold you up with my victorious right hand.

ISAIAH 41:10

As soon as I pray, you answer me;
you encourage me by giving me strength.

PSALM 138:3

When you begin to see the obstacles in your life as opportunities for God to show his power, they will not seem so overwhelming. The very hardships and weaknesses that challenge and frighten you may be the tools God will use to make you stronger and help you fight life's battles better. When you pray, it mysteriously and miraculously allows our limitless God to work in your situation regardless of your own limitations. In what areas have you been pushed to the limit this week?

Is God taking you beyond your limits in order to work in your life?

Focus on His Power

Jesus looked at them intently and said,
"Humanly speaking, it is impossible.
But with God everything is possible."

MATTHEW 19:26

When you try to cope with problems in your own strength, you are easily overwhelmed. When you focus on God in the midst of problems, you become aware of his power and stop being preoccupied with yourself and your limitations.

You can cope with anything when God's strength replaces your weakness. Your impossibilities are God's opportunities.

If you were to give your biggest problems
to God, how might he use them as
opportunities to do something big through you?

Faith Impresses God

*He takes no pleasure in the strength of a horse
or in human might. No, the LORD's delight
is in those who fear him, those who put
their hope in his unfailing love.*

PSALM 147:10-11

God is more impressed by your faith than your abilities. He uses your abilities only in proportion to your faith in him. Your abilities give you the potential to do good; faith gives you the power to do good.

Neither potential nor power alone is sufficient; they must work together in harmony. If you want to delight God, say yes to him, step out in faith, and watch him accomplish great things through you!

*Are you limiting your potential by trusting
in your abilities more than you trust in God?
What could happen today if you exercised your
limited abilities with an unlimited faith in God?*

Your Reactions Matter

Don't be surprised at the fiery trials you are going through, as if something strange were happening to you. Instead, be very glad—for these trials make you partners with Christ in his suffering, so that you will have the wonderful joy of seeing his glory when it is revealed to all the world.

1 PETER 4:12-13

Sometimes the suffering you experience is not your fault. We live in a fallen world where sin is often allowed to run its course, affecting both the godly and ungodly.

Your reaction to suffering and your perspective of how God uses suffering in your life are critical. God doesn't want to see you suffer, but the great message of the Bible is that God promises to bring renewal, healing, and spiritual maturity through suffering. Then you will be stronger and better equipped to help others, lead others, and live with purpose and meaning.

What good can come from your suffering?

Life's Greatest Goal

People will come from all over the world—from east and west, north and south—to take their places in the Kingdom of God. And note this: Some who seem least important now will be the greatest then, and some who are the greatest now will be least important then.

LUKE 13:29-30

Obeying God is life's greatest goal. It keeps you focused on what is really important, leads you in God's will, and gives you an eternal perspective that affects the way you live on earth and guarantees your future in heaven.

If you drift away from obeying God, your daily choices will become selfish, and you will begin to feel cynical and dissatisfied. But if you make obeying God your first priority, he will give you an eternal perspective on your daily activities and a greater desire to obey him as you see the rewards of doing so.

How much of an eternal perspective do you bring to your daily choices?

Influence Others
for Christ

*Let your good deeds shine out for all to see,
so that everyone will praise your heavenly Father.*

MATTHEW 5:16

A leader who is a Christian is in a special position to influence others for Christ.

If you claim to be a follower of God, make sure others can truly see that you are following him.

They too will want to follow God if they like what they see in your life.

———— • ————

Are you following God close enough that those who are following you can see God as well?

God's Wisdom Is the Best Advice

To those who listen to my teaching, more understanding will be given, and they will have an abundance of knowledge.

MATTHEW 13:12

In an age of conflicting claims and confusing directions, everyone is looking for good advice. Maybe that's why counselors are in such great demand and advice columns are in every newspaper.

But there is a critical difference between wise counsel and well-meaning advice. God's wisdom is the best counsel because he is all-knowing. First seek advice from the One who knows everything that will happen tomorrow and the next day and every day to come. Then you can better measure and interpret the advice you receive from others.

How can you make a habit of seeking advice from God's Word?

Spiritual Goals

I am certain that God, who began the good work
within you, will continue his work until
it is finally finished on the day when
Christ Jesus returns.

PHILIPPIANS 1:6

Don't you realize that in a race everyone runs,
but only one person gets the prize?
So run to win! ... We do it for an eternal prize.
So I run with purpose in every step.

1 CORINTHIANS 9:24-26

The biblical concept of maturity is pictured as reaching the finish line or completing the task. We should mature as individuals, growing to become the kind of people who are exemplary and productive. We should mature as Christians, striving for and reaching the spiritual goals God gives us. Maturity is growing in Christ toward the finish line of life and giving that process everything you have.

Have you set any goals for spiritual maturity?
If not, how do you know you are growing?

Build Others Up

*We should help others do what is right
and build them up in the Lord.*

ROMANS 15:2

*Be joyful. Grow to maturity. Encourage each other.
Live in harmony and peace. Then the God
of love and peace will be with you.*

2 CORINTHIANS 13:11

God promises to be with those who encourage each other and who build others up. When you build others up, you affirm the gifts God has given them. And when they use those gifts properly, they fulfill the purpose for which they were created.

You can play a role in releasing God's gifts in others by building them up. Then God will help you in every way he can.

*Who can you encourage
today by building them up?*

Faith to Overcome

Do not be afraid of the terrors of the night,
nor the arrow that flies in the day.
Do not dread the disease that
stalks in darkness, nor the disaster that
strikes at midday. ... The LORD says,
"I will rescue those who love me.
I will protect those who trust in my name."

PSALM 91:5-6, 14

When your problems and obstacles consume you, you often give in to fear—fear that you will fail, fear that you will let others down, fear that God will not help you when you need it most.

Fear tempts you to focus on the size of your problem rather than on the size of your God. Focus on God in faith, and you will sense him fighting by your side to overcome the obstacles in front of you.

Do you approach the obstacles in
your life with fear or with faith?

Answer God's Call

*Don't copy the behavior and customs of this world,
but let God transform you into a new person
by changing the way you think. Then you
will learn to know God's will for you, which
is good and pleasing and perfect.*

ROMANS 12:2

When God is calling you to a specific task, he will keep interrupting your thoughts. Your heart will long to do what God wants you to do. You will know it is what you should do.

When you answer his call, opportunities to serve him will follow again and again. Seize those moments, and answer God's call. Don't let the windows of opportunity close, or you may miss what God has in store for you.

---

*Are you listening for God's call
and answering when you hear it?*

Bring His Love to the World

You will receive power when the Holy Spirit comes upon you. And you will be my witnesses, telling people about me everywhere ... to the ends of the earth.

ACTS 1:8

Many of us fear being called into ministry. We think that being in ministry means we have to move to some remote third-world country and learn another language. Although that may be the ministry God has in mind for some, there are countless other ways you can be involved in ministry.

Ministry is bringing the love of Christ to those who need it, and it is the job of every Christian. God promises that he will equip you with what you need to show his love to others and help bring them into a relationship with him.

How do you participate in God's ministry?

Share in His Compassion

The LORD *is good to everyone. He showers
compassion on all his creation.*

Compassion is a tearing of the heart, a true caring,
a deeply emotional response to someone in need.
Compassion can be a litmus test of our commitment and desire to love others as Christ loves us. To
be Christlike is to share in his compassion toward the
needy and those who cannot help themselves.

If you are not moved by the incredible needs and
hurts of the people around you, you are in danger of
developing a heart of stone, which could become too
hard to respond to others or even to God. Remember
the Lord's compassion to you, then pass it along to
those around you.

*Is your heart becoming warmer
and more compassionate or colder
and harder toward others in need?*

Choose Honesty and Purity

Who may climb the mountain of the LORD?
Who may stand in his holy place?
Only those whose hands and hearts are pure,
who ... never tell lies.
They will receive the LORD's blessing and have
a right relationship with God their savior.

PSALM 24:3-5

Honesty creates trust, and trust is the basis of all relationships. God wants you to be completely honest—with him, with others, and with yourself.

You do not honor God if you cheat or lie to get ahead. When you are honest in every detail of your life, you will have a clear conscience, earn the trust and respect of others, and receive God's blessing.

Make the decision to be honest and pure, and God promises to bless you.

If others were asked to describe you,
would they call you an honest person?

Have a Servant's Heart

Among you it will be different.
Whoever wants to be a leader
among you must be your servant.

MATTHEW 20:26

If you want others to look up to you, then have a servant's heart, be willing to take responsibility for your actions instead of passing the buck when it's convenient, speak up when you see something that is wrong, and never seek glory for yourself.

The world teaches people in authority to look and act in control, to step on the people under their authority, and to bend the rules instead of playing fair. But in the end, the people who have shown kindness, integrity, humility, and a deep love for God will be the most respected and honored.

Are you living by God's definition
of authority or by the world's?

The Necessity of Change

*Put on your new nature, and be renewed
as you learn to know your Creator
and become like him.*

COLOSSIANS 3:10

God is in the business of change. Leaders are also in the business of change. One of your primary tasks is initiating, responding to, and managing change. Whether it's helping others change raw materials into a finished product, change ignorance into knowledge, or change political or social structures, leaders need to understand both the necessity of change and the tensions that come with it.

As you deal with change, remember how God is changing you to be more like him. You will discover new effectiveness in your work and relationships.

*How do you manage change
in your role as a leader?*

A Firm Foundation to Lead

Elijah the prophet walked up to the altar and prayed, "O LORD, God of Abraham, Isaac, and Jacob, prove today that you are God in Israel and that I am your servant. Prove that I have done all this at your command. O LORD, answer me! Answer me so these people will know that you, O LORD, are God."

1 KINGS 18:36-37

A leader's confidence in God can literally change everything. Elijah's boldness on Mount Carmel marked the beginning of the liberation of God's people from the wicked influence of Baal worship.

When you have confidence in God and his principles for living, you will have a firm foundation from which to lead, inspire those who follow you, liberate them from unhealthy practices, and ensure the positive results of godly living.

How can you lead with more confidence?

Reflect God's Goodness

*A good person produces good things from
the treasury of a good heart, and an
evil person produces evil things from
the treasury of an evil heart.*

MATTHEW 12:35

What you say and do opens a window to your soul and shows everyone around you what is inside.

If you practice the goodness you have received from God, others will see treasures within.

If you don't, the bad things you say and do will reveal the impoverishment of your soul.

*Can others see a treasury
of goodness inside of you?*

Apply the Truth

*All Scripture is inspired by God and is useful
to teach us what is true and to make us realize
what is wrong in our lives. It corrects us when we
are wrong and teaches us to do what is right.*

2 TIMOTHY 3:16

*Your regulations remain true to this day,
for everything serves your plans.*

PSALM 119:91

If everyone did whatever they wanted, it wouldn't be long before chaos and anarchy would take over. There must be some rules, some laws that people must follow in order for any society to function well. Thus, there must be some absolute truths, set in place from the beginning of time, that apply to all people in all times and all places. God promises that when people live by these absolutes, which are found in his Word, individual lives will function better and society as a whole will be a place of order and peace.

*Could you make a list of ten absolute
truths you should be living by?*

No Limits to God

"My thoughts are nothing like your thoughts,"
says the LORD. "And my ways are far beyond
anything you could imagine."

ISAIAH 55:8

God often does the opposite of what we might expect. He chose David, the youngest rather than the oldest son of Jesse, to be king of Israel. He took Saul of Tarsus, the most vicious opponent of the early church, and transformed him into Paul, the greatest missionary of all time.

He took the cross, an object of death and ultimate defeat, and made it the sign of victory over sin and death for all eternity. Don't limit God to your own understanding and expectations. The Father wants to surprise you in ways that inspire your awe, love, gratitude, and joy.

In what ways do you expect little
from God? How can you expect
more than you dreamed possible?

Trust His Guidance

*Your word is a lamp to guide my feet
and a light for my path.*

PSALM 119:105

If we could see the future, we'd likely become scared of the hard times ahead or proud of our accomplishments. God's guidance is not like a searchlight that brightens a broad area; instead, it's more like a flashlight that illuminates just enough of the path ahead to show you where to take the next step.

God has a definite plan for you, but he usually doesn't reveal it all at once. He wants you to learn to trust him each step of the way.

*In what area can you trust God's guidance
today by taking one step forward?*

FEBRUARY

Be Kind

Sympathize with each other. Love each other as brothers and sisters. Be tenderhearted, and keep a humble attitude. Don't repay evil for evil. Don't retaliate with insults when people insult you. Instead, pay them back with a blessing.

1 PETER 3:8-9

While it's good to have big goals for your family life or career or personal achievements, it's also important to set smaller daily goals. Being kind toward others, being humble, doing good to someone who takes advantage of you, reading your Bible, saying a kind word—these are small goals that add up to great accomplishments when you practice them throughout your lifetime.

God promises to bless you for these small acts of obedience to him, for they are the building blocks of the bigger things God wants you to accomplish.

What small goals can you set for yourself today?

Scripture Shapes Character

All Scripture is inspired by God and is useful to teach us what is true and to make us realize what is wrong in our lives. It corrects us when we are wrong and teaches us to do what is right.

2 TIMOTHY 3:16

Scripture not only shapes leaders, it also gives leaders the method for shaping the people they lead.

God's Word shows you the path for your personal spiritual journey, reveals when you sin and stray, rebukes you to return you to the right way, and teaches you how to live in the power of the Spirit and remain faithful.

Leaders who intentionally teach, discipline, and disciple using clear direction from God's Word will shape people in the most effective, productive way.

———•———

How effectively are you using God's Word to lead others?

Focus on the Biblical Truths in Scripture

Anyone who wanders away from this teaching has no relationship with God. But anyone who remains in the teaching of Christ has a relationship with both the Father and the Son.

2 JOHN 1:9

If you don't focus on the road when you're driving, you risk running off of it, putting your life in great danger. In the same way, if you don't focus on the path clearly mapped out for you in God's Word, you risk drifting off the road that will lead you safely to life's most important destination.

Be careful to focus on the truths you read in Scripture and to listen to godly wisdom. Paying attention to the caution signs your heavenly Father gives you will ensure safer travel on your journey through life.

How can you keep your "spiritual eyes" focused on the road in front of you?

Work to Please God

*My life is worth nothing to me unless
I use it for finishing the work assigned
me by the Lord Jesus.*

ACTS 20:24

*I take joy in doing your will, my God,
for your instructions are written on my heart.*

PSALM 40:8

You don't need to do earthshaking things in order to have a meaningful life. Your life has meaning when you do the work God has given you to do, whether it is coaching a Little League team, running a company, or evangelizing the world.

When you work to please the Father, your life has meaning because you are sharing his love with everyone in your circle of influence.

How can you find meaning in your work today?

Spiritual Gifts

*Just as our bodies have many parts
and each part has a special function,
so it is with Christ's body.
We are many parts of one body,
and we all belong to each other. ...
If God has given you leadership ability,
take the responsibility seriously.*

ROMANS 12:4-5, 8

God assigns everyone a unique role based on the abilities he gives them and the needs of his church.

It is important for you to discover the specific gifts God has given you and how to use those gifts to serve him. One of the gifts he has given you is leadership ability. Use this gift wisely, and you will reach your full God-given potential as well as help others reach their potential.

*What other spiritual gifts has God
given you besides leadership abilities?*

Exercise Your Faith Muscles

My health may fail, and my spirit may grow weak, but God remains the strength of my heart; he is mine forever.

PSALM 73:26

Just as your muscles get stronger the more you exercise them, so your faith gets stronger the more you exercise it.

Spend time in training with God each day, being careful to obey his regimen for healthy, godly living.

Then your faith will be strengthened and your spiritual muscles will be ready to take on whatever life throws at you.

———•———

Do you have a spiritual training plan to strengthen your faith?

Bring Out the Best in Others

Accept each other just as Christ has accepted you so that God will be given glory.

ROMANS 15:7

You have a great deal of influence over others, for better or for worse. Use your influence positively and accept others for who they are. Don't be quick to judge. Don't accept only those people who are like you or who are important or who are popular. Welcome everyone in the way Jesus Christ would welcome them.

It isn't a matter of searching out the best people to be around; it's a matter of bringing out the best in the people God has brought to you. Then God will be glorified because you will recognize that the way he treats people brings out the best in everyone.

—————— • ——————

Do you know someone who does not feel accepted by others? What can you do to affirm and encourage that person?

Encourage Others through Your Words

Don't use foul or abusive language.
Let everything you say be good and helpful,
so that your words will be an encouragement
to those who hear them.

EPHESIANS 4:29

There are few things as powerful as encouragement. Every day, the words you speak to others will determine whether they will be inspired and motivated to take on new challenges or whether they will be discouraged and deflated to the point of doing nothing more than required.

As a leader, your words determine the dramatic difference between the two outcomes. When you encourage others, you can inspire them to greatness and effectiveness.

How can you encourage others
today through your words?

Courage Stretched Out

*If we are faithful to the end, trusting God
just as firmly as when we first believed,
we will share in all that belongs to Christ.*

HEBREWS 3:14

Perseverance can be defined as "courage stretched out." Although God sometimes delivers his people from difficult or painful circumstances, he often calls us to courageous and enduring faithfulness in the midst of trials.

Perseverance is obeying God and following his way even when it doesn't seem to make sense or produce immediate results. Consistent obedience develops perseverance.

How have you seen the relationship between obedience and perseverance in your life?

Quality Depends on Your Attitude

Love is patient and kind. Love is not jealous or boastful or proud or rude. It does not demand its own way. It is not irritable, and it keeps no record of being wronged. It does not rejoice about injustice but rejoices whenever the truth wins out. Love never gives up, never loses faith, is always hopeful, and endures through every circumstance.

1 CORINTHIANS 13:4-7

Your quality of life depends more upon your attitude than your circumstances. Your attitude makes the difference between being content and happy or being discontent and miserable.

When you focus on loving and serving God and the people around you, you will develop an eternal perspective that will change your attitude about life in this world.

Have you had a bad attitude lately? Practice loving others as described in today's Bible promise, and see how your attitude changes.

Passing the Faithfulness Test

If we are unfaithful, he remains faithful,
for he cannot deny who he is.

2 TIMOTHY 2:13

Who are you really, deep down inside? Do you really love others? Are you really faithful to your family, friends, and coworkers? Faithfulness is necessary to maintain love because even those closest to you will disappoint you at times.

But God loves you and remains faithful to you even when you disappoint him with your sin and rebellion. Model that same love to others and remain faithful to them even when they fail you. Then you will show your love to be genuine, and those you lead will know that you truly care.

Are you passing the test of faithfulness?

Love with Purpose

We do know that we will be like him.

1 JOHN 3:2

Confidence comes from the realization and assurance that the Father loves you, that he has given you specific talents and gifts, that he wants you to use those gifts for him, and that he has given you salvation and eternal life in heaven.

Knowing these truths gives you complete confidence that your life has meaning now and into eternity.

---

*How can you live with meaning
and purpose today because of
your confidence in God's promises?*

Romance

*Surely your goodness and unfailing love will
pursue me all the days of my life,
and I will live in the house of the LORD forever.*

PSALM 23:6

Romance is the language of love that fosters intimacy with another person. What a wonderful feeling when someone expresses their affection for you, enjoys your company, and is captivated by you! As you read the Bible, you learn that God himself is a romantic who desires an intimate relationship with you. He desires your company and is interested in the smallest details of your life. He wants nothing more than to walk with you through this life and for all eternity.

As you realize how precious and valuable you are to God, you will find confidence in your faith, strength to be faithful to him, and a deep desire to know him better.

*What can you learn from God
about romance and love?*

Love like Christ

I am giving you a new commandment:
Love each other. Just as I have loved you,
you should love each other.
Your love for one another will prove
to the world that you are my disciples.

JOHN 13:34-35

Loving others as Christ loves us is an act of spiritual maturity that comes when we realize the eternal significance of every person God has created. When you learn to see others as God sees them, you will be able to love even those you dislike or who dislike you. Love isn't about receiving gifts or having pleasurable experiences. Love isn't about what you get out of it. Genuine love is willing to sacrifice, even to the point of death, for the good of others. Are you willing to give up your very life so that someone else might come to know Jesus? If you can answer yes, it is because of the love of God at work in you.

How can you learn to love as Jesus loves?

Gentleness Is Powerful

*You should clothe yourselves instead
with the beauty that comes from within,
the unfading beauty of a gentle and quiet spirit,
which is so precious to God.*

1 PETER 3:4

Being gentle does not mean that you are a doormat or let others walk all over you. God is the perfect example of gentleness, yet he is also a mighty warrior who is able to defeat the powers of hell.

In God's eyes, gentle people are the most powerful and influential people in the world because they make an impact on others without the use of force and without conflict.

Gentleness may be your most powerful weapon of influence because you can accomplish much more by gentleness than by coercion.

———•———

*Have you made developing the
quality of gentleness a top priority?*

The Spirit Intercedes

The Holy Spirit helps us in our weakness.
For example, we don't know what God wants
us to pray for. But the Holy Spirit prays
for us with groanings that cannot
be expressed in words.

ROMANS 8:26

The Holy Spirit lives within each believer and gives wisdom, discernment, and guidance. This amazing gift of God's own presence within you gives you direction and helps you when you need it most. Don't neglect this gift. The more sensitive you are to the promptings of the Holy Spirit, the closer you will be to God and the more life will make sense.

Even when you don't know how to express yourself to God, the Holy Spirit promises to pray for you and articulate your thoughts and feelings to God. What a comfort to know that God's Holy Spirit is praying for you!

How strong is the influence of the Holy Spirit
in your life? How can you become more
sensitive to the Spirit's promptings?

Created for Purpose

God created human beings in his own image.
In the image of God he created them;
male and female he created them.

GENESIS 1:27

Dignity is the worth and significance that every human being has been given because we are created in the image of God. Unfortunately, our sinful human nature causes us to assign each other differing values of either importance or insignificance.

When you have a proper view of human dignity, you will be motivated to fulfill God's purpose for you as well as help others find and achieve God's purpose for them. Then you will respect others and build them up rather than rank them beneath you.

Do you have a high view of human dignity?

How does the way God sees
you affect how you see others?

Make Good Choices

*The instructions of the LORD are perfect,
reviving the soul. The decrees of the
LORD are trustworthy, making wise the simple.*

PSALM 19:7

God is the perfect source of wisdom. He promises to make his wisdom available to help you make good choices. He shares his wisdom with you through the Holy Spirit, the Bible, your own conscience, and godly advice.

The closer you walk with God, the easier it will be to make wise choices. Immerse yourself in God's Word and in prayer, and surround yourself with godly people. You will find the wisdom to determine the right thing to do.

How can you grow in wisdom?

Receive God's Forgiveness

If you forgive those who sin against you,
your heavenly Father will forgive you.
But if you refuse to forgive others,
your Father will not forgive your sins.

MATTHEW 6:14-15

The stress and tensions of leadership mean there will be conflicts and problems between leaders and the people they lead.

Wise leaders make sure that candid confession and genuine forgiveness are a way of life for their group or organization. These leaders set the tone of reconciliation with believers and nonbelievers alike.

They understand and live out the clear teaching of God's Word that we receive God's forgiveness only when we forgive others.

How can you set an example of forgiveness
for those around you to follow?

Small Choices
Test Character

If you are faithful in little things,
you will be faithful in large ones.
But if you are dishonest in little things,
you won't be honest with greater responsibilities.
And if you are untrustworthy about
worldly wealth, who will trust you with
the true riches of heaven?

LUKE 16:10-11

Your character is tested in the small choices you make. Cheating in a little thing is cut out of the same piece of cloth as cheating in a big way. Just as a small drop of dye will color even a large glass of clear water, a small act of deception colors your whole character.

The Father promises that when you are honest and faithful in small ways, he will give you more and greater opportunities to do good.

What are the little things that
will test your character today?

Humility Is True Greatness

*Anyone who becomes as humble as this
little child is the greatest in
the Kingdom of Heaven.*

MATTHEW 18:4

The less you seek to honor yourself, the more God will honor and bless you. Pride builds barriers that keep God out of your life. Humility opens the way for God to work in you because it makes you willing to seek his help and honor him for it.

Pride reaches no further than your own ego. Humility is true greatness because its effects reach into the Kingdom of Heaven.

———— • ————

Is practicing humility a priority for you?

Putting Others First

*[Jesus] called the twelve disciples over to him,
and said, "Whoever wants to be first must
take last place and be the servant
of everyone else."*

MARK 9:35

Arrogance is dangerous because it causes you to spend more and more time trying to meet your own needs, and less and less time meeting the needs of others. According to Jesus, however, leadership involves meeting the needs of others first.

Arrogance focuses you inward and causes you to neglect the people you lead. The more you humbly put others ahead of yourself, the more God will lift you up.

*In what areas are you most likely to
become arrogant by putting your
needs ahead of the needs of others?*

Your On-Call Advisor

Don't worry about anything; instead,
pray about everything. Tell God what you
need, and thank him for all he has done.
Then you will experience God's peace,
which exceeds anything we can understand.
His peace will guard your hearts and
minds as you live in Christ Jesus.

PHILIPPIANS 4:6-7

With all the worries and crises that often face leaders, it's hard to remember that in times of panic, the Father is your on-call advisor whom you can consult anytime.

Train yourself to pray, even if only a quick prayer, the instant that panic hits you. Prayer keeps you connected to God's power and wisdom, which give you instant insight into managing crises and overcoming the paralysis of panic.

How often do you consult with God each day?

Prepared for Crisis

*[Jesus said,] "Here on earth you will have
many trials and sorrows. But take heart,
because I have overcome the world."*

JOHN 16:33

Crisis should not surprise you. You should expect
to encounter difficulties because we live in a fallen
world. Jesus even tells us that we will have problems
here on earth.

His words of warning should keep you from pan-
icking when crisis hits. And his promise of victory
should keep you from becoming discouraged or feeling like there is no way out.

Are you prepared for a crisis?

Follow Christ's Example

Take a new grip with your tired hands and
strengthen your weak knees. Mark out
a straight path for your feet so that
those who are weak and lame will not
fall but become strong.

HEBREWS 12:12-13

Everyone is an example of something to someone else. We all follow the example of others, and we all set an example for others.

The Bible promises that the way you live influences other people, and not just in matters of daily living; you can influence others for good or evil, for Christ or Satan.

What kind of example have you been exhibiting to others?

If the people you lead follow your
example, will they be following Jesus?

Compassion Builds Loyalty

*He will rescue the poor when they cry to him;
he will help the oppressed, who have no one
to defend them. He feels pity for the weak and
the needy, and he will rescue them. He will
redeem them from oppression and violence,
for their lives are precious to him.*

PSALM 72:12-14

Leaders can honor God and others through acts of compassion. Godly leaders show the same kind of compassion to others that God has shown to them.

Compassion reveals that you have a gracious heart, generosity, and integrity. When you show compassion, it builds loyalty and security among those you lead.

---

*How can you incorporate compassion
into your leadership style?*

Praying for Others

You are helping us by praying for us.
Then many people will give thanks because
God has graciously answered so many prayers.

2 CORINTHIANS 1:11

Intercession is the practice of praying for the needs of others. The Bible promises that praying for others makes a difference.

It is easy to become discouraged if you think there is nothing anyone can do to help you with a particular problem—or nothing you can do to help someone else who needs it. But the most important thing you can do for others and others can do for you is to pray.

In ways beyond our understanding, intercessory prayer opens the door for the love and power of God to come through. Praying for others also causes you to care more about them.

For whom can you intercede today?

Controlled by the Spirit

Letting your sinful nature control your mind leads to death. But letting the Spirit control your mind leads to life and peace.

ROMANS 8:6

When you let the Holy Spirit control your life, he will bring you peace of heart and mind. Letting the Spirit take control means being willing to give up those things that you most want to control.

When you try to accomplish everything you want and control the outcomes, you usually end up feeling unsatisfied. But if you let him, God's Holy Spirit will show you what he wants you to get done each day, and that will be enough. What satisfaction that brings!

Do you like to feel in control? Think about what controls your mind and heart, and find some ways to let the Holy Spirit control your life more.

MARCH

Always a Way Out

*The temptations in your life are no different
from what others experience. And God is
faithful. He will not allow the temptation to be
more than you can stand. When you are tempted,
he will show you a way out so that you can endure.*

1 CORINTHIANS 10:13

The Bible teaches that one of Satan's main goals is to tempt you to sin—although your own selfish appetites certainly make the Tempter's work easier. Just as blood attracts a shark, so your weaknesses attract Satan's attacks.

The key is to identify where you are most vulnerable—where you have the greatest tendency to sin. Then ask God to strengthen you in those areas. He promises to help you fight and endure the temptations when Satan attacks you again.

*In what area of your life are you
most tempted to do wrong?*

A Living Stone

*You are living stones that God is
building into his spiritual temple.*

1 PETER 2:5

All of God's people make up his church. Jesus Christ is the foundation and the cornerstone of the church, and each believer is a "living stone" that not only supports the others around it but also plays an important role in the design and function of the church.

You are just one living stone, but God promises that you are exactly where he wants you and you are an essential part of his church.

Don't ever think that your place in God's church is insignificant.

*How does it make you feel to be
one of the stones God has chosen
and placed in the building of his church?*

Knowing Right from Wrong

My child, don't lose sight of common sense
and discernment. Hang on to them,
for they will refresh your soul.
They are like jewels on a necklace.
They keep you safe on your way,
and your feet will not stumble.

PROVERBS 3:21-23

Discernment is the ability to differentiate between right and wrong, true and false, good and bad, important and trivial, godly and ungodly. Discernment helps you properly interpret issues and understand the motives of people who might have a certain agenda. Discernment shows you the way through the maze of options you face. When you practice discernment and train yourself to detect right from wrong, you can avoid the pitfalls and confusion so many people fall into. God promises that discernment will keep you safe in the way that he wants you to go.

How can you practice better discernment?

Recognize the Miracles

"Yes," says the LORD,
"I will do mighty miracles for you ..."

MICAH 7:15

It is hard for us to imagine the parting of the Red Sea or manna appearing from heaven. The miracles recorded in the Bible can seem like ancient myths if we fail to recognize God's intervention in our lives today. Just as Pharaoh was blind to God's miracles, which were performed right before his eyes through Moses, we, too, are sometimes blind to God's miracles when we fail to notice the mighty works he is doing all around us.

When we look for God, he shows himself in miraculous ways: in the birth of a baby, in a new cure for a deadly disease, in an awesome sunset. God still works miracles. He is able—and willing—to do the impossible in order to help us do his work. This means that no situation is hopeless. God encourages us to pray big prayers, to never lose hope, and to look for miracles every day.

What miracle are you looking for today?

Upon a Rock

Upon this rock I will build my church, and all the powers of hell will not conquer it.

Matthew 16:18

Despite all the bad news and all the bad press, the church is still the Father's people. It is a community for worshiping God, supporting fellow believers, and learning who God is and how to live out the Christian faith.

God will always use the church as his divine instrument to proclaim his message of salvation and to wage war against the forces of evil.

He promises that the church will never disappear and can never be overcome.

Do you have as much confidence in the church as God does?

The Presence of Purity

Now he has reconciled you to himself through
the death of Christ in his physical body.
As a result, he has brought you into his
own presence, and you are holy and blameless
as you stand before him without a single fault.

COLOSSIANS 1:22

Holiness is much more than the absence of sin; it is the presence and practice of righteousness, purity, and godliness. Holiness means being wholly dedicated and devoted to God, being distinct and separate from the world's way of living, and being committed to right and pure living.

When you became a Christian, God made you holy by forgiving your sins. He now looks at you as though you have never sinned. But you have not yet perfected the practice of holiness. You must strive each day to be holy, to be more like Jesus. Striving for holiness is a lifelong process because you will not be completely holy until you get to heaven.

How can you practice holiness in your life today?

Courage to Carry On

"I hold you by your right hand—
I, the LORD your God. And I say to you,
'Don't be afraid. I am here to help you.'"

ISAIAH 41:13

It's natural to be afraid when you are completely alone in a frightening place or in difficult circumstances. But it's not so scary when you are with a friend. Walking with the Lord God, who holds the universe in his hands, should give you courage.

When you face troubled times, never forget that God remains with you. He gives you his love and his comfort and the courage to go on.

How can you depend on God to give
you courage in frightening circumstances?

Stop the Excuses

*"Lord," Gideon replied, "how can I rescue Israel?
My clan is the weakest in the whole tribe of
Manasseh, and I am the least in my entire family!"
The LORD said to him, "I will be with you."*

JUDGES 6:15-16

Gideon thought he had a good excuse to get out of serving God. But the qualifications God looks for are different from what we might expect.

God often chooses the least likely people to do his work in order to demonstrate his mighty power more effectively.

If you know God has called you to do something, stop trying to excuse yourself. He promises to give you the help and strength you need to get the job done.

*Are you making excuses to get out
of something God wants you to do?*

Wise Stewardship

*These are the gifts Christ gave to the church:
the apostles, the prophets, the evangelists,
and the pastors and teachers. Their responsibility
is to equip God's people to do his work and
build up the church, the body of Christ.*

EPHESIANS 4:11-12

Good leaders understand that delegation is not simply getting out of work or dumping the tasks you don't want to do on others. Leaders are to develop others who can develop others.

Delegation is necessary for everyone involved: for the leaders, for those who serve with the leaders, and for those who are being served.

Without delegation, leaders are overburdened, helpers are underutilized, and people are underserved. God promises that good delegation results in wise stewardship of everyone's time and resources.

---

*What task can you delegate that
will help someone else to grow as
well as help you be more effective?*

A Sense of Purpose

The seed on the rocky soil represents those who hear the message and immediately receive it with joy. But since they don't have deep roots, they don't last long. They fall away as soon as they have problems or are persecuted for believing God's word.

MATTHEW 13:20-21

Those who lack depth have no place for the seeds of God's Word to grow. Without that depth, the hot sun of persecution or problems will cause their belief to wither. Their sense of purpose fades, and along with it, their relationship with God.

As your relationship with God deepens, your enthusiasm for your tasks grows and thrives under God's care and provision. The best way to increase your motivation is to tend to your relationship with the Father.

*Have you lost all motivation?
How deep is your relationship with God?*

Mighty Things

With God's help we will do mighty things.

PSALM 60:12

Yes, I am the vine; you are the branches.
Those who remain in me, and I in them,
will produce much fruit.
For apart from me you can do nothing.

JOHN 15:5

At the most basic level, to accomplish something means to complete a task, whether it is washing up the dishes or winning the Super Bowl. The Bible describes many tangible accomplishments, but it also highlights spiritual accomplishments, which we so often overlook.

A spiritual accomplishment might be having an active prayer life, maturing in the faith, telling a neighbor about Jesus, gaining victory over temptation, or offering a word of encouragement. God promises that these kinds of accomplishments do the greatest good and bring the greatest rewards.

What will you try to accomplish today?

Friends Are
Wonderful Gifts

*If we are living in the light, as God is in the light,
then we have fellowship with each other,
and the blood of Jesus, his Son,
cleanses us from all sin.*

1 JOHN 1:7

Good friends are a wonderful gift, and fellowship among believers is even more wonderful because the living God promises to be in their midst. Christians have a common perspective on life because they know their sins have been forgiven, and it affects their present and their future. Christian fellowship provides a place for honest sharing, for encouragement to stay strong in the face of temptation and persecution, and for supernatural help in dealing with problems. Christian leaders also need Christian fellowship to help them stand strong in their convictions and model healthy relationships.

*Are you in regular fellowship
with other Christians?*

Reach Out

I will be your God throughout your lifetime—
until your hair is white with age.
I made you, and I will care for you.
I will carry you along and save you.

ISAIAH 46:4

The God who made you shows his care for you by protecting, providing, and preserving. You can share God's care with others by doing the same for them. You can protect by being kind, helpful, and willing to reach out.

You can provide by giving of your time, treasure, and talents to those in need. You can preserve by helping to maintain harmony through your words and actions.

Is there someone God has put in
your path who needs your care today?

Aligned Prayers

*If you remain in me and my words remain
in you, you may ask for anything you want,
and it will be granted!*

JOHN 15:7

As you maintain a close relationship with God by consistently studying his Word, your prayers will begin to line up with his will.

When that happens, God is delighted to grant your requests.

*What do you often ask God for?
Are your prayers aligned with his will for you?*

Take Time Out

We are merely moving shadows, and all our busy rushing ends in nothing. We heap up wealth, not knowing who will spend it.

PSALM 39:6

Don't confuse busyness with accomplishment. A schedule that is too full may reflect a lack of wise priorities.

If you are too busy, you don't have time to do anything well or to enjoy the fruits of your labor.

Ceaseless activity without real purpose will sap the energy and meaning from your life and leave you feeling frustrated.

How often do you say, "I'm too busy"? What can you do to change that?

The Power of God

With God's help we will do mighty things.

PSALM 60:12

Don't look at the size of the problem, but at the size of your all-powerful God.

When there are great things to be done, you have a great God who will do them through you.

Ask him what he wants you to accomplish with his power at work in your life.

How can you rely on God's power today?

He Is Right Beside You

Listen to the LORD who created you. ...
"Do not be afraid, for I have ransomed you.
I have called you by name; you are mine.
When you go through deep waters,
I will be with you. When you go through
rivers of difficulty, you will not drown.
When you walk through the fire of oppression,
you will not be burned up; the flames
will not consume you."

ISAIAH 43:1-2

The circumstances of your life cannot separate you from God. Your hard times don't get in God's way.

In fact, those are the times when God's promise to be with you is most clearly revealed through his infinite love and care for you.

———— • ————

When tough times come, are you
sure that God is right beside you?

Patience to Do God's Will

Patient endurance is what you need now,
so you will continue to do God's will.
Then you will receive all that he has promised.

HEBREWS 10:36

It takes patience to do God's will. In fact, you can't do God's will without it because God's will doesn't happen all at once; it unfolds over time. As you pass each test of your faith, you will develop patience for when God asks you to take the next step of faith.

Impatience may cause you to rush ahead and take matters into your own hands. At first you trust that God will handle the situation, but when his solution seems slow in coming, you decide that God needs a bit of help. Instead of rushing ahead, you must learn to trust God completely, even if it means having to wait.

Do you have the patience to let
God's will unfold one day at a time?

The Creative Wonder of God

The heavens proclaim the glory of God.
The skies display his craftsmanship.
Day after day they continue to speak;
night after night they make him known.

PSALM 19:1-2

God the Creator is a God of design, color, plan, organization, beauty, magnificence, and orderliness. The finest model of craftsmanship and artistic skill is found in the creation of the universe. Creativity is the overflow of a heart and mind filled with the good things of God.

If you need a little inspiration or motivation, try filling your heart and mind with the creative wonders of God. See how it inspires you to find new and fresh ways to express yourself.

How can the workmanship of
God spark your own creativity?

A Fulfilling Life

Oh, the joys of those who do not follow the advice
of the wicked, or stand around with sinners,
or join in with mockers.
But they delight in the law of the LORD,
meditating on it day and night.
They are like trees planted along the riverbank,
bearing fruit each season. Their leaves never wither,
and they prosper in all they do.

PSALM 1:1-3

Obedience is the way to a fulfilling and productive life. When you obey God and his Word, you will have a clear conscience and uninterrupted fellowship with him. When you are closely connected to God, you will honor and respect others and want to work with them rather than against them.

Then you will be spending your time and energy on the things that last, the things God values. That is how obedience will bring you joy.

———— • ————

How might you be filled with
joy as you obey God today?

Open the Door for Healing

People who conceal their sins will not prosper, but if they confess and turn from them, they will receive mercy. Blessed are those who fear to do wrong, but the stubborn are headed for serious trouble.

PROVERBS 28:13-14

Saying "I'm sorry" for something you have done wrong is one of the most difficult things to do. You have to recognize your fault, face it head-on, and then humble yourself enough to admit it to someone else.

Offering a simple apology demonstrates that you are willing to open the door to healing and blessing. If you want to experience peace and growth in your relationships with friends, coworkers, or God himself, the practice of admitting you are wrong will help you reach a new level of trust and respect. The act of apologizing is also a powerful example to others.

Is there someone you need to apologize to? How might your apology benefit both of you?

A Shining Example

God has united you with Christ Jesus.
For our benefit God made him to
be wisdom itself. Christ made us
right with God; he made us pure
and holy, and he freed us from sin.
Therefore, as the Scriptures say, "If you
want to boast, boast only about the LORD."

1 CORINTHIANS 1:30-31

Ultimately you should be known not for what you have done but for what God has done through you and for you.

Your purpose is to be a shining example of God's greatness and goodness. Then you will have the privilege of knowing that God is pleased to accomplish his good works through you.

Are you more interested in being known
for your own accomplishments or for
what God accomplishes through you?

Coming to God

If we confess our sins to him, he is faithful and just to forgive us our sins and to cleanse us from all wickedness.

1 JOHN 1:9

At the name of Jesus every knee should bow, in heaven and on earth and under the earth, and every tongue confess that Jesus Christ is Lord, to the glory of God the Father.

PHILIPPIANS 2:10-11

Confession is both acknowledging guilt and proclaiming allegiance to Jesus Christ.

Confession is a necessary part of coming to God, being freed from sin, and being identified as a follower of Jesus.

It is also a necessary part of knowing God, knowing others, and allowing others to know you.

Is confession an important part of your leadership style?

God Blesses the Just

Be just and fair to all. Do what is right and good,
for I am coming soon to rescue you and
to display my righteousness among you.
Blessed are all those who are careful to do this.

ISAIAH 56:1-2

Justice is important because it ensures fairness, equality, consistency, and equal opportunity to all. True justice eliminates politics, double standards, inequity, and oppression.

Justice comes from the heart of God, which is why God blesses people who are just.

Leaders who insist on justice, fairness, and equity in their followers or their organization will experience blessing from God.

Is justice essential in your leadership?

Opposition

I cry out to the LORD; I plead for the LORD's mercy.
I pour out my complaints before him and
tell him all my troubles. When I am overwhelmed,
you alone know the way I should turn.
Wherever I go, my enemies have set traps for me.

PSALM 142:1-3

Sometimes you face overwhelming opposition; you feel outnumbered and helpless. God boosts your confidence by reminding you that just as he has delivered his people from their enemies in the past, he will deliver you from your troubles.

You can have courage in the face of opposition when you know that God is stronger than your worst problem and that he wants to use his strength to help you. God promises to be with you, and his power is available to you when you do what pleases him.

What opposition are you facing?
Have you asked God to help you overcome it?

Draw Close to Him

He gives power to the weak and strength to the powerless. Even youths will become weak and tired, and young men will fall in exhaustion. But those who trust in the Lord will find new strength. They will soar high on wings like eagles. They will run and not grow weary. They will walk and not faint.

ISAIAH 40:29-31

One of the best ways to reduce burnout is to take time out to be close to God. When you're burning the candle at both ends, you are likely neglecting your time with God. When you draw close to him, you can tap into his power, strength, peace, protection, and love.

Schedule time each day to meditate on his Word and on other writings that challenge you spiritually. As you focus on God's priorities, your priorities will become clearer.

How can you make time for God in your busy schedule?

Doubt Can Grow Faith

*When doubts filled my mind, your
comfort gave me renewed hope and cheer.*

PSALM 94:19

Virtually every biblical hero struggled with doubts about God or God's ability or desire to help. God doesn't mind when you doubt as long as you continue to seek him in the midst of it. Doubt can become sin if it leads you away from God and into skepticism, cynicism, or hard-heartedness.

But God does promise that doubt can become a blessing if your honest searching leads you to a better understanding of God and a deeper faith in him. When others see your hope in God even as you struggle with doubt, they will be inspired to follow your example and cling to their faith no matter what their circumstances.

*When you find yourself doubting God,
do you let it move you closer
to him or farther away?*

God Blesses Faithfulness

Commit everything you do to the LORD.
Trust him, and he will help you.

PSALM 37:5

Commitment to God is more than intellectual agreement with his principles. Commitment involves giving your whole self—body, soul, emotions, and mind—for his use.

It requires a decision of the mind followed by an act of the will to follow through, regardless of the difficulty or the cost.

Commitment to God can be costly, but God promises to help you and bless you when you are faithful to him.

On a scale from one to ten, what is your level of commitment to God?

A Generous Heart

*"Bring all the tithes into the storehouse so there
will be enough food in my Temple. If you do,"
says the LORD of Heaven's Armies,
"I will open the windows of heaven for you.
I will pour out a blessing so great you won't
have enough room to take it in!"*

MALACHI 3:10

Old Testament law made it clear that God wanted his people to tithe—to give him the first tenth of their income—to demonstrate their obedience and trust that he would provide for them. When Jesus came, he made it clear that he loves a cheerful giver. This means that he loves a generous heart.

The principle of the tithe is a good place to start when setting an example of generosity for those you lead. It demonstrates concern for those in need, commitment to being a part of God's work in the world, and sacrifice by giving up something in order to give more to others.

*What steps can you take to
give more generously to others?*

Giving Your Best to God

*Work willingly at whatever you do, as though
you were working for the Lord rather than
for people. Remember that the Lord will
give you an inheritance as your reward,
and that the Master you are serving is Christ.*

COLOSSIANS 3:23-24

While it may seem overwhelming to give your best in everything for God, this is the kind of attitude that God promises to reward.

As you give God your best in your quiet times with him, he will energize you through prayer and his Word. When you give your heavenly Father your best from your income, you will be blessed as you see how it can help others.

And when you give God your best in serving others, you will be blessed with personal satisfaction as well as deeper relationships. God turns your best efforts into eternal rewards.

How can you give your best to God today?

Bring God Joy

*The LORD your God will delight in you if you
obey his voice and keep the commands and
decrees written in this Book of Instruction,
and if you turn to the LORD your God with
all your heart and soul.*

DEUTERONOMY 30:10

Can finite, sinful human beings truly bring joy and delight to the Lord, the Creator of the universe? God says yes.

He created you because he wants to have a relationship with you, to delight in being with you. But a good relationship works in both directions.

A relationship that brings joy to God is built on trust, regular communication, honesty, humility, service, and unconditional love. These are the traits that will make your leadership effective as well.

Do you think you are bringing God joy?

APRIL

Value in God's Eyes

*Whoever wants to be first must take
last place and be the servant of everyone else.*

MARK 9:35

True greatness comes from finding your real value in God's eyes. That is why humility is the essence of true greatness. Don't be fooled into striving to gain everything you desire in this world at the cost of eternal rewards in heaven.

If the greatest benefactor of your achievements is yourself, then you are trying to find meaning in the wrong way.

*Are you living as if what you do is more
important than who you are before God?*

Take a Risk

When you work in a quarry, stones might fall and crush you. When you chop wood, there is danger with each stroke of your ax.

ECCLESIASTES 10:9

Do not be afraid of the terrors of the night, nor the arrow that flies in the day. Do not dread the disease that stalks in darkness, nor the disaster that strikes at midday.

PSALM 91:5-6

Life is filled with risks. The person who never takes any risks never succeeds, never enjoys everything life has to offer, and never fully experiences God's plan. You are too cautious if you let fear control you to the point where any risk seems too great.

Fear keeps you from taking risks at all. Caution keeps you from risking too much. Obedience to God balances the two.

Do you need to take more risks to obey God?

Hope to Endure

Because God raised Jesus Christ from
the dead ... we live with great expectation,
and we have a priceless inheritance—
an inheritance that is kept in heaven for you,
pure and undefiled, beyond the reach of change
and decay. ... There is wonderful joy ahead,
even though you have to endure
many trials for a little while.

1 PETER 1:3-6

Just as focusing on a fixed point in the distance helps you go in a straight line, followers of Jesus should fix their eyes on the eternal horizon in order to move straight toward their ultimate goal of heaven.

There you will live with God forever without pain or sorrow or suffering. This hope for eternity enables you to endure the challenges and discomforts of daily life here on earth. It gives you the motivation and energy to press on in your daily tasks. Your hope offers an eternal perspective on life to those you lead.

How does your hope for eternity
change the way you lead today?

Use Your Opportunities

God says, "At just the right time, I heard you.
On the day of salvation, I helped you."
Indeed, the "right time" is now.

2 CORINTHIANS 6:2

Today when you hear his voice,
don't harden your hearts.

HEBREWS 3:15

Do you ever think that your plan is better than God's or that his plan is just too inconvenient for you? Realize that God's call deserves and requires an immediate response.

He does not ask you to do anything without giving you the resources and power to accomplish it. If you avoid the opportunities God gives you, you will miss his blessings as well. If you accept his call, you will be living according to his will, which will bring you great blessing and joy.

Have you received a clear call from God?
Will you avoid it or accept it?

Be Willing to Trust

I tell you the truth, those who listen to my message and believe in God who sent me have eternal life. They will never be condemned for their sins, but they have already passed from death into life.

Faith is more than just believing; it is entrusting your very life to what you believe. For example, you may *believe* that someone can cross a deep gorge on a tightrope. But would you *trust* that person to carry you across? If you truly had faith, you would say yes.

Faith in God means that you are willing to trust him with your whole life. You are willing to follow his guidelines for living, as outlined in the Bible, because you have the conviction that his will is best for you.

You are even willing to endure ridicule and persecution for your faith because you are sure that God is who he says he is and he will keep his promises about salvation and eternal life in heaven.

How can you strengthen your faith today?

Inspiration from the Resurrection

Jesus told her, "I am the resurrection and the life. Anyone who believes in me will live, even after dying."

JOHN 11:25

Jesus' resurrection is the key to the Christian faith. Why? Because just as he promised, Jesus rose from the dead. You can be confident, therefore, that God will keep all of his other promises. And you can be certain of your own resurrection because God has power over death.

The resurrection of Jesus is the basis of your faith because by it he proved to be more than just a good human leader; he showed that he is the Son of God, who brings eternal life to all who believe in him. Let his resurrection inspire you to lead not just with human abilities but with the spiritual qualities that come from your living Lord.

How does Jesus' resurrection affect your perspective on this life and your leadership?

Prepared for Heaven

Our present troubles are small and won't last very long. Yet they produce for us a glory that vastly outweighs them and will last forever!

2 CORINTHIANS 4:17

As a heaven-bound follower of Jesus, you need to put heaven and earth in proper perspective. Here on earth, you will live for a hundred years or less. In heaven, a hundred *million* years is just the beginning!

Yet God has determined that how you live during your short time on earth will prepare you for heaven.

This gives you purpose in your life, perspective on your troubles, and anticipation for what God has planned for you in eternity.

---

*How does your view of
heaven affect your life now?*

Serve Others First

*I appeal to you, dear brothers and sisters,
by the authority of our Lord Jesus Christ,
to live in harmony with each other.
Let there be no divisions in the church.
Rather, be of one mind, united in thought
and purpose. ... God has united you
with Christ Jesus.*

1 CORINTHIANS 1:10, 30

Unity of heart, purpose, and mind comes when everyone strives for the same things—serving others first and helping others before helping themselves. Nothing creates more division than selfishness and the desire to get what you want at the expense of other people.

But when everyone's goal is to serve others, then everyone's needs will be met. When you as a leader model the priority of serving others first, you will see unity blossom in your organization.

*What five things can you
do to serve others today?*

Mercy Every Day

*You, O Lord, are a God of compassion
and mercy, slow to get angry and filled
with unfailing love and faithfulness.*

PSALM 86:15

Receiving mercy is one of the best experiences in the world. God not only showed you mercy by forgiving your sins when you became a Christian, he forgives you and shows you mercy every day, 365 days a year.

Only God could be that patient and merciful! Receive his mercy with a grateful heart, and commit yourself to extending the same kind of mercy to others.

*Is there someone who might need to
receive mercy today instead of judgment?*

Your Heart Matters

The LORD doesn't see things the way you see them.
People judge by outward appearance,
but the LORD looks at the heart.

1 SAMUEL 16:7

Appearance matters, but make sure you're looking at the right things. It's not wrong to pay attention to how you look or how you present your work or your organization to others. Just don't neglect your spiritual appearance, which is more important.

It's easy to get distracted by appearances, whether your own or someone else's. But you can have an incredible impact when other people look right past your outward appearance because of what they see on the inside—God himself shining through you.

God promises that the inward condition of your heart is what matters to him.

———•———

Do you focus more on your outward
appearance or on what God sees inside of you?

Invest in Heaven

Teach those who are rich in this world not to be proud and not to trust in their money, which is so unreliable. Their trust should be in God, who richly gives us all we need for our enjoyment. Tell them to use their money to do good. They should be rich in good works and generous to those in need, always being ready to share with others. By doing this they will be storing up their treasure as a good foundation for the future so that they may experience true life.

1 TIMOTHY 6:17-19

Investing money can be a tool for blessing or a trap for deception. The secret to investing is knowing whom to trust and where to invest.

Use the resources God has given you to do good for others; then your investments will never lose their value. The only lasting investment comes from trusting in God and investing in helping others.

Where are you investing your greatest treasures?

Giving Generously

*Remember this—a farmer who plants only
a few seeds will get a small crop. But the one
who plants generously will get a generous crop.*

2 CORINTHIANS 9:6

You should not give in order to get more, but your resources often grow when you do give more. Perhaps this is because the qualities that make you generous also make you responsible and trustworthy.

But another important reason is that God in his grace often entrusts more to you so that you will be a greater channel of his blessings to others.

Too often people think of rewards only in terms of money, but the spiritual rewards you receive for your generosity are far more valuable than money.

*What intangible gifts have you
received when you have given generously?*

He Accepts You

No power in the sky above or in the earth below—
indeed, nothing in all creation will ever be
able to separate us from the love of God
that is revealed in Christ Jesus our Lord.

ROMANS 8:39

It's entirely appropriate for an employer or supervisor to disapprove of an employee's work if it does not meet certain standards. In the same way, it is entirely appropriate for God to disapprove of your behavior if you are enjoying a lifestyle that is contrary to his commandments.

We all need and long for the kind of approval that is not based on performance, and only God's unconditional love can fulfill that need. You are a child of God, created in his image, so he loves and accepts you not for what you've done but for who you are. Knowing that there's nothing you can do to cause him to love you less should give you peace of mind and motivate you to please him even more.

How does God's unconditional love change
the way you show your approval of others?

Perfect in His Sight

Our bodies are buried in brokenness, but they will be raised in glory. They are buried in weakness, but they will be raised in strength. They are buried as natural human bodies, but they will be raised as spiritual bodies. ... For our dying bodies must be transformed into bodies that will never die.

1 CORINTHIANS 15:43-44, 53

Your resurrected body will be a physical body like you have now, but it will also have supernatural characteristics. You may be able to walk through walls, as Jesus did with his resurrected body. Most important, your new body will never deteriorate because of the effects of sin. You will never be sick or in pain again, and your mind will never think sinful thoughts. You will be fully and finally perfect in God's sight. When you show your confidence in this truth as you live out your daily life, you will inspire those you lead.

Are you living each day with confidence in the resurrection?

Entrust the Future to Him

That is what the Scriptures mean when they say, "No eye has seen, no ear has heard, and no mind has imagined what God has prepared for those who love him." But it was to us that God revealed these things by his Spirit. For his Spirit searches out everything and shows us God's deep secrets.

1 CORINTHIANS 2:9-10

God promises to reveal enough of the future to give you hope. You know there is a heaven, you know how to get there, and you know that your future in heaven will be more wonderful than you can imagine.

Perhaps knowing more details than that would be too much for anyone to take in. God wants you to trust him and demonstrate your belief that what he promises will happen. Your trust in God for the future will be an inspiration and an example to others.

What details about the future do you need to entrust to God?

Never Defeated

*We are pressed on every side by troubles,
but we are not crushed. We are perplexed,
but not driven to despair. We are hunted down,
but never abandoned by God. We get knocked
down, but we are not destroyed.*

2 CORINTHIANS 4:8-9

Defeat is common to all people, so it keeps you connected with the realities faced by everyone. Failing from time to time keeps you humble and dependent on God.

If you were to win all the time, your character would have no chance to grow. You might become proud, arrogant, or shallow, and rely only on yourself without regard for the opinions or the help of others.

If you let God help you, he promises to use times of defeat to strengthen your character and keep you humbly dependent on him.

*How might God give you victory
even when you experience defeat?*

Pray for Peace

Turn away from evil and do good.
Search for peace, and work to maintain it.
The eyes of the LORD watch over those who
do right; his ears are open to their cries for help.

PSALM 34:14-15

As Christians, we are called to work and pray for peace in the world. This only happens as more people make peace with God and truly understand what his peace means.

When you pursue peace with others, God promises to be actively involved in your life. Why? Because people who pursue peace are pursuing God's own agenda.

With God's help and a commitment to peace, you can make a difference in a world that desperately needs God's peace.

———————•———————

Is pursuing peace—in your own relationships
and in the world—on your agenda?

Talk to God Often

My sheep listen to my voice;
I know them, and they follow me.

JOHN 10:27

We keep in touch with people because it is vital to the quality and success of our relationships, whether in marriage, friendships, family relations, or business partnerships. The same principle applies to your relationship with God.

You must find ways to communicate with him and learn to listen as he communicates with you. Good communication allows you to experience a breakthrough in your spiritual life.

The more time you spend communicating with God, the closer and more successful your relationship with him will be.

Are you in touch with God? How much time
do you spend communicating with him?

Don't Deny Your Emotions

The Holy Spirit produces this kind of fruit in our lives: love, joy, peace, patience, kindness, goodness, faithfulness, gentleness, and self-control.

GALATIANS 5:22-23

We often think of emotions negatively because they tend to get out of control. But without emotions, you could not experience the power and satisfaction of a relationship with God, nor could you model the character of God in your life. Don't deny your emotions, but don't let them control you or cause you to sin.

Allow the emotions God has given you to deepen your relationship with him. They will help you experience the drama and power of Christian living, which will also have a profound impact on those you lead.

Which emotions help you feel closer to God?

Be Good to Others

*If you are wise and understand God's ways,
prove it by living an honorable life, doing good
works with the humility that comes from wisdom.*

JAMES 3:13

There's nothing wrong with desires and passions, as long as they are good and healthy. But too often we let sinful desires linger in our minds, and then they creep down into our hearts. You can resist bad thoughts and wrong desires by spending more time doing good deeds.

Living out God's goodness is a proactive way to curb your sinful desires and encourage your passion for serving God and others. Influencing the character of others, which is an important part of leadership, requires that goodness—in thoughts and actions—is an integral part of your daily life.

*How can you plan to live
out God's goodness today?*

A Desire to Obey

When you obey my commandments,
you remain in my love, just as I obey
my Father's commandments and remain
in his love. I have told you these things
so that you will be filled with my joy.
Yes, your joy will overflow!

JOHN 15:10-11

Young children often try to obey their parents because they want to please them, although a child's obedience is not always perfect. That is the same attitude God is looking for in you. He knows that because of your sinful nature, you won't always obey him. What he wants is your desire to obey because that is a sign that you love and respect him and believe his way is best.

When you want to obey God and do your best to follow his commands, many of the people you lead will want to follow your example.

How great is your desire to obey God?

The Ultimate Sacrifice

Just as each person is destined to die once and after that comes judgment, so also Christ died once for all time as a sacrifice to take away the sins of many people. He will come again, not to deal with our sins, but to bring salvation to all who are eagerly waiting for him.

HEBREWS 9:27-28

In the Old Testament, God's people offered sacrifices to him as part of their worship. The blood of an animal was shed as a substitute for the punishment the people deserved for their sin. All the sacrifices of the Old Testament anticipated the ultimate sacrifice of God's own Son, Jesus, on the cross for the sins of the world.

Whenever you must sacrifice or give up something, you can be reminded in some small way of God's greatest sacrifice and his promise of eternal life in heaven because of it.

What can you sacrifice today to remind you of Jesus' greatest sacrifice?

Comfort in His Presence

Jesus said, "Come to me, all of you who are weary and carry heavy burdens, and I will give you rest."

MATTHEW 11:28

When tragedy strikes or problems overwhelm you, do you wonder what happened to God? Do you wonder why he would allow these things to happen?

Nagging doubts might cause you to question whether God still loves you. When you lose confidence that God cares about you, you are in danger of pushing him away and separating yourself from your only source of hope.

When tough times come, move immediately toward God, not away from him. You will receive comfort and gain perspective.

Do you still believe that God cares about you even when trouble comes your way? How can you learn to expect his comfort instead of doubting his presence?

Holiness Brings Peace

*Now I entrust you to God and the message
of his grace that is able to build you up and
give you an inheritance with all those he
has set apart for himself.*

ACTS 20:32

Living a life of holiness has countless practical benefits. It brings peace and confidence into your life, as well as freedom from addiction and guilt.

It brings you into closer fellowship with the heavenly Father and comes with the promise of an eternal inheritance in heaven.

All of these things help you lead with greater confidence, maturity, and perspective.

———— • ————

*When you work hard at living a holy life,
how will it affect those you lead?*

A Conductor of His Power

God is working in you, giving you the desire and the power to do what pleases him.

PHILIPPIANS 2:13

Even though the awesomeness of God's power cannot be fully understood, we do know that his power is available to all who believe in him. Thankfully, God's power does not depend on human strength or power. In fact, your own resources can get in the way if you rely on them instead of on God.

God's power flows through you, especially your weaknesses, just as an electric current flows through a wire. The wire is simply a conductor; it has no power in itself. But without the wire, the current doesn't go anywhere. God is looking for people who are willing to be wired for his service. If you are willing to be a conductor of his power, he promises to do amazing things through you.

Have you tapped into God's power?

A Matter of Faith

This Good News tells us how God makes us right
in his sight. This is accomplished from start
to finish by faith. As the Scriptures say,
"It is through faith that a righteous person has life."

ROMANS 1:17

Salvation is truly the greatest of accomplishments, but ironically it is not accomplished through your own work—it only comes through the work of God in your heart.

Salvation is simply a matter of faith, of believing that Jesus Christ died for your sins so that you can live forever with him in heaven. Thank God for accomplishing this tremendous work in you!

Have you shared your life's greatest
accomplishment with those you lead?

A Wholesome Balance

Physical training is good, but training for godliness is much better, promising benefits in this life and in the life to come.

1 TIMOTHY 4:8

God cares deeply about the condition of both your body and your soul. Spiritual exercise should be as purposeful and strenuous as physical exercise. But remember that the benefits of spiritual fitness last for eternity, while the benefits of physical fitness last only as long as your body.

Knowing the eternal benefits of spiritual exercise should motivate you to keep your physical and spiritual health in wholesome balance and help you experience a vibrant relationship with your Creator.

Are you getting enough spiritual exercise?

He Will Fight for You

Do not be afraid! Don't be discouraged by
this mighty army, for the battle is not yours,
but God's. ... Do not be afraid or discouraged.
Go out against them ... for the LORD is with you!

2 CHRONICLES 20:15-17

The people of Judah could see only a vast enemy army, not their God standing by to destroy it. It's easy to focus on your problems and forget that God is near and ready to help. Be careful to separate your feelings of discouragement from the facts of reality: Discouragement can cause you to doubt God's love and care, drawing you away from your greatest source of help.

Realize that God will fight on your behalf and help you succeed when you see that he is right beside you.

Do you sometimes feel as if an enemy
army is lined up against you? How can you
let go and let the Lord fight your battles?

Take Caution

Keep watch and pray, so that you will not give in to temptation. For the spirit is willing, but the body is weak.

Satan is constantly on the attack, trying to tempt you to sin against God. You will give in from time to time—everyone does.

When you throw caution to the wind, you give in to temptation at every turn, and you are in danger of becoming completely ineffective for God.

But when you take caution, you learn to be aware of temptation so that you can recognize it, fight it, and avoid it in the future.

What are some ways you can exercise caution in the face of temptation?

Respond with Prayer

You have heard the law that says,
"Love your neighbor" and hate your enemy.
But I say, love your enemies!
Pray for those who persecute you!

MATTHEW 5:43-44

Showing love to your enemies seems completely unreasonable—unless you realize that you were an enemy of God until he forgave you. When you love your enemy, you see that person as Christ does—someone in need of grace and forgiveness. Getting to that point takes prayer.

When you pray for someone, you can't help but feel compassion for them. When you respond with prayer and blessing instead of retaliation when someone hurts you, God promises to bless you. God can even turn your enemy into your friend.

———————•———————

How can you show love to your enemies?

MAY

He Is Changeless

*Jesus Christ is the same yesterday,
today, and forever.*

HEBREWS 13:8

*God is working in you, giving you the desire and
the power to do what pleases him.*

PHILIPPIANS 2:13

Change is one of the constants of life. Some changes are positive: a new friend, a new house, a financial windfall. Other changes are negative: the loss of a loved one or a job, the upheaval of a natural disaster. Either way, change is stressful.

The Bible offers two truths about change: First, despite the changing world around us, God is changeless and dependable. Second, God wants an inner change of heart, called repentance, that produces an outward change of lifestyle, called obedience. When you change your heart, you will change your life forever.

---

*Are you changing by becoming more like
your changeless and dependable God?*

Clear Direction for Decisions

Show me the right path, O LORD; point out the road for me to follow. ... The LORD is good and does what is right; he shows the proper path to those who go astray. He leads the humble in doing right, teaching them his way.

PSALM 25:4, 8-9

Knowing Scripture and gleaning its wisdom will give you clear direction in your decision-making and provide you with the discernment you need to make healthy choices.

The right choice is the one that is consistent with the principles and truths found in God's Word.

How often do you turn to the Bible when evaluating your choices?

Adversity Shapes You

Be truly glad. There is wonderful joy ahead, even though you have to endure many trials for a little while. These trials will show that your faith is genuine. It is being tested as fire tests and purifies gold—though your faith is far more precious than mere gold. So when your faith remains strong through many trials, it will bring you much praise and glory and honor on the day when Jesus Christ is revealed to the whole world.

1 PETER 1:6-7

The stories of God's people in the Bible testify that being faithful to God does not eliminate adversity. But these heroes of the faith also testify that adversity molds and shapes you into a stronger, better, spiritually richer person—and that is cause for joy.

When you look at adversity this way, you will be a powerful example to those you lead.

How can you be truly glad in all of the circumstances you will face today?

He Intercedes for You

The Holy Spirit helps us in our weakness.
For example, we don't know what God wants
us to pray for. But the Holy Spirit prays for us
with groanings that cannot be expressed in words.
And the Father who knows all hearts knows what
the Spirit is saying, for the Spirit pleads for us
believers in harmony with God's own will.

ROMANS 8:26-27

When you are in such grief and confusion that you don't even know how to express it to God, the Holy Spirit prays for you and expresses your feelings for you. When you can't even form the words of a prayer, let the Holy Spirit intercede for you.

He will pray for you when you can't even pray for yourself. He will implore God to give you the comfort you so desperately need.

How does it comfort you to know
that the Holy Spirit is praying for you?

Godly Desires

I will give you a new heart,
and I will put a new spirit in you.
I will take out your stony,
stubborn heart and give you a tender,
responsive heart.

EZEKIEL 36:26

When you commit your life to God, he gives you a new heart, a new nature, and a new desire to please him. When God stirs your heart, your desires will be in line with his so that what you want to do will be what he wants you to do.

God's will for you becomes your greatest desire. There is nothing more wonderful than having your desires match God's!

Are you taking full advantage of
the new heart God has given you?

Jesus' Authority Means Love

Jesus came and told his disciples, "I have been given all authority in heaven and on earth. Therefore, go and make disciples of all the nations, baptizing them in the name of the Father and the Son and the Holy Spirit. Teach these new disciples to obey all the commands I have given you.

MATTHEW 28:18-20

If a king boldly proclaimed his complete authority, what would you expect him to do next? Probably eliminate his enemies, seize control of his assets, and make his subjects fear him. How different it was for Jesus.

After announcing his absolute authority over all things, Jesus commands his followers to make disciples—in other words, to encourage others to follow him, not by coercion but out of love.

How are you using the authority God has given you?

God's Great Reversal

*Whoever wants to be first must take last place
and be the servant of everyone else.*

For a Christian, greatness is measured in ways the world often misses. As a leader, this means that you must adjust your expectations according to the Father's criteria.

When leaders measure themselves or others by worldly standards of greatness, they miss God's will. God's "great reversal," in which the last will be first and the first will be last, fools many who buy into the world's system.

*Do you have plans for greatness?
Do those plans need some adjustments
to fit God's view of greatness?*

Admit Your Failures

Each time he said, "My grace is all you need.
My power works best in weakness."

2 CORINTHIANS 12:9

One thing is certain: You must learn to live with failure. In fact you must embrace it because it is in your failures that God's power works best in you. Everyone has weaknesses. Everyone fails—a lot.

The key to success is not the number of times you fail but the way you respond to failure. Those who admit their failures can look forward to an extra measure of God's strength to help them through their failures and on to greater things.

* * *

The next time you fail, look forward to
God releasing more of his power in your life.

First Place

*Looking at the man, Jesus felt genuine love for him.
"There is still one thing you haven't done,"
he told him. "Go and sell all your possessions
and give the money to the poor, and you
will have treasure in heaven.
Then come, follow me."*

MARK 10:21

God challenges you to examine your heart and make sure he has first place in your life.

Your faith will mature through genuine examination and careful attention to God's commands.

He promises eternal rewards to those who are willing to sacrifice their very life to follow him.

*What are some of the ways
God is challenging you?*

Stay on Course

Jesus told him, "Anyone who puts a hand to the plow and then looks back is not fit for the Kingdom of God."

LUKE 9:62

Distractions take your focus off Jesus. You might be doing great things, but if you take your eyes off Jesus, even for a moment, you could stumble. God's enemies work hard to distract you. They will try everything to get your mind off of God and onto sin. If temptation can turn your head even for a minute, it puts you in danger of swerving off the path of righteousness.

Many other things can distract you from your walk with God—busyness, material things, problems, even good things. If you are aware of these distractions, you can try to minimize them so you stay on course in following God.

How can you minimize the distractions that keep you from focusing on the road God wants you to take?

Making an Impact

*Praise the LORD! How joyful are those who fear
the LORD and delight in obeying his commands.
Their children will be successful everywhere;
an entire generation of godly people
will be blessed ... and their good
deeds will last forever.*

PSALM 112:1-3

The Lord blesses those who strive to be faithful.
And because God is so generous, his blessings flow
beyond those faithful ones to other people as well.
As you walk faithfully with God, his blessings will
extend to those you live and work with.

Then you can see how a group of passionate people who are faithful to God can make an enormous
impact on the world around them.

Is your faithfulness to God rubbing off on others?

Guarding Your Heart

Guard your heart above all else,
for it determines the course of your life.

PROVERBS 4:23

Be careful to guard your heart against temptation because your heart is the center of your desires and affections. Your heart is especially vulnerable because it is easily swayed by emotion, and emotions aren't always rational.

If you are caught up in the emotions of the moment, your heart might urge you feed those feelings, even if it leads you to do something wrong.

God promises that guarding your heart will lead you in the way you should go.

———— • ————

In what area is your heart most vulnerable?
How can you protect it from giving in
to the wrong things?

Make a Difference

*Fix your thoughts on what is true, and honorable,
and right, and pure, and lovely, and admirable.
Think about things that are excellent
and worthy of praise. Keep putting
into practice all you learned.*

Life is less confusing when you realize and accept that God truly is in control. The purpose of God's control is not to manipulate you or order you around but to assure you that this world is not random and chaotic. If that were the case, life would be utterly meaningless.

But because God is in control of the world, you can be sure his promises will come true. You can live a life of purpose rather than confusion and make a difference for all eternity. Then you will be at peace.

---

*Do you really believe that God is in control?
If so, how can you spend more time thinking
about him rather than the things you can't control?
How might this increase your peace of mind?*

The Standard for Truth

*Jesus said to the people who believed in him,
"You are truly my disciples if you remain
faithful to my teachings. And you will know
the truth, and the truth will set you free."*

JOHN 8:31-32

One of the key responsibilities of a leader is to define truth. You help the people you lead develop a worldview and a perspective that enables them to interpret life from the eternal vantage point of God's truth. Even when it's hard to take, the truth sets people free from ignorance and deception.

Jesus is truth, and he sets the standard for truth. Follow his truth, and you will be free from the false promises that enslave so much of the world.

*Where do you find truth? What truths
are you communicating to others?*

Be Different

Jesus replied, "But even more blessed are all who hear the word of God and put it into practice."

LUKE 11:28

Faith alone is enough for salvation, but your behavior provides evidence that your faith is genuine. Leaders have a greater responsibility to model godly behavior because many people are watching to see if God has truly transformed them. If your sinful behavior doesn't change after you become a Christian, then people will wonder if your confession of faith is really genuine.

Have you asked the Father to forgive your sins, come into your life, and transform you from the inside out? When people see godly behavior in you, they will want to know what motivates you, what makes you different. Then you will have a wonderful opportunity to tell them about your faith in God, and he will bless you for it.

Can others see Jesus when they look at your behavior?

Thought-Controlled Living

*Those who are dominated by the
sinful nature think about sinful things,
but those who are controlled by the Holy Spirit
think about things that please the Spirit.*

ROMANS 8:5

While the human imagination is powerful, it is also limited and can be hijacked for sinful purposes. Because it is connected to your thought life, your imagination is controlled by what controls your thoughts.

When selfish desires and sinful pleasures control your mind, your imagination becomes a tool of destruction, producing lustful fantasies or meaningless daydreams. But when your thoughts are controlled by the Holy Spirit, your imagination is inspired by God's creative nature and becomes a tool of innovation and vision.

What have you been imagining lately?

At the Center

*Jesus said to the people who believed in him,
"You are truly my disciples if you remain
faithful to my teachings. And you will know
the truth, and the truth will set you free."*

JOHN 8:31-32

As a leader, it is your responsibility to keep God's truth at the center of everything you do and every decision you make. Then you will be doing what is wise and approved of by God.

The utmost importance of the Father's truth applies whether you are the leader of a family, a church group, or a large corporation.

Is God's truth at the center of your leadership?

From a Godly Perspective

"My thoughts are nothing like your thoughts,"
says the Lord. "And my ways are far beyond
anything you could imagine."

ISAIAH 55:8

Assumptions made from a human viewpoint lead to actions made from a human viewpoint—and that can close the door to God's miracles in your life.

When you are open to the possibilities of God's ways, you begin to see more clearly how he is at work all around you.

God promises to work in your life, but you must see things from his perspective or you could be blind to what he is doing in and through you.

* * *

Do you have assumptions about God
or about your life that need to be
changed to match God's point of view?

Fasting

*When you fast, comb your hair and wash your face.
Then no one will notice that you are fasting,
except your Father, who knows what you
do in private. And your Father, who sees
everything, will reward you.*

MATTHEW 6:17-18

Fasting is abstaining from things that you regularly enjoy in order to give greater attention to spiritual concerns. It is one of the most frequently illustrated spiritual exercises in Scripture, practiced in a variety of situations.

Fasting has been described as praying with the body. God promises that when you fast, you will be rewarded. Fasting feeds the soul. It is a significant way to develop spiritual power and a more immediate sense of God's presence.

*Have you ever considered fasting?
Make it a goal to try it this week,
and prepare yourself for the profound
experience of coming closer to God.*

God's Way Is Best

*Do what is right and good in the LORD's sight,
so all will go well with you.*

DEUTERONOMY 6:18

The right thing to do is the smart thing to do. God's commandments are not burdensome obligations but pathways to joyful, meaningful, satisfying lives. God's demand for obedience comes out of his desire for your well-being.

Since God is the Creator of life, he knows how life is best lived. Obedience demonstrates your willingness to follow through on what God says to do.

Obedience shows how much you trust that God's way is best for you.

* * *

*Do you see obedience as a burdensome
obligation or as the pathway to the best life?*

Let Him Rescue You

Call on me when you are in trouble, and I will rescue you, and you will give me glory.

PSALM 50:15

We are most severely tested in times of crisis because there are so many things out of our control.

Allow crises to become a means for the heavenly Father to rescue you, to reveal his care and his power working on your behalf.

———— • ————

Can the people within your sphere of influence see that you trust God in times of crisis?

Serve Where He Leads

All of you, serve each other in humility, for
"God opposes the proud but favors the humble."

1 PETER 5:5

Humility is a prerequisite for service. True humility results from understanding who you are and who God is. Humility allows you to serve wherever God places you and do whatever God asks of you. When you are sick or injured and must rely on a physician's care, you are humbled because you realize your vulnerability.

Likewise, you are humbled when you realize you are completely dependent on God to heal your soul. When you have this kind of humility, you will be happy to serve your Lord in any way he asks.

Do you have the humility to serve wherever
God is calling you, even if few people notice?

Set Healthy Boundaries

God's discipline is always good for us,
so that we might share in his holiness.
No discipline is enjoyable while it is happening—
it's painful! But afterward there will be
a peaceful harvest of right living
for those who are trained in this way.

HEBREWS 12:10-11

Failing to stay within God's boundaries brings painful consequences every time—guaranteed. It makes life harder than it needs to be.

When you remember the struggles you've faced in the past as a result of stepping outside God's boundaries, it will help you avoid repeating your mistakes.

Learning from your mistakes is part of a pattern of right living that will bless you and those you love and lead.

What consequences have you faced because
you stepped outside of God's boundaries?

Rest to the Weary

It is a permanent sign of my covenant. ...
For in six days the LORD made heaven
and earth, but on the seventh day
he stopped working and was refreshed.

EXODUS 31:17

I have given rest to the weary.

JEREMIAH 31:25

Why would the omnipotent God of the universe rest after his work of creating the world? Surely it wasn't because the Almighty was physically tired! Rather, we see that God, in ceasing from his work, called rest holy. God knows that we, too, need to cease from our work to care for our spiritual needs.

Work is good, but you must balance it with regular worship and attention to the health of your soul. God promises that you will be refreshed if you carve out regular times for worship and spiritual nourishment.

Are you getting enough rest?

Play Your Unique Part

*All of you together are Christ's body,
and each of you is a part of it.*

1 CORINTHIANS 12:27

He makes the whole body fit together perfectly.

EPHESIANS 4:16

Christ created you with unique gifts to contribute to the church, the body of Christ. The human body is made up of different parts, yet all the parts are compatible and work together to sustain life. It is the same with the church.

Each believer is a separate part with a unique role to play. Your role is different from the roles of others. But the beauty of these differences is that they help sustain the body of Christ and allow it to flourish. God promises that differences within the body of believers actually enhance the church's productivity and compatibility.

*How can you use your unique
gifts and the unique gifts of
others to increase effectiveness?*

You Have Been Chosen

*God saved us and called us to live a holy life.
He did this, not because we deserved it,
but because that was his plan from
before the beginning of time—to show us his
grace through Christ Jesus.*

2 TIMOTHY 1:9

God has both a general purpose and a specific purpose for you. In a general sense, you have been chosen by God to let the love of Jesus shine through you to make an impact on others.

More specifically, God has given you unique spiritual gifts and wants you to use them to make a worthwhile contribution within your sphere of influence. The more you fulfill God's general purpose for you, the clearer your specific purpose will become.

*Are you fulfilling the purpose God
has for you by letting Jesus' love
shine through you to help others?*

Honesty Matters

If you are faithful in little things, you will be faithful in large ones. But if you are dishonest in little things, you won't be honest with greater responsibilities.

LUKE 16:10

Honesty matters greatly to God because it reveals your character. If you can't be trusted to be honest in a small matter, how can you be trusted to be honest in bigger things? That's why honesty is the test for responsibility.

When you have built your life on honesty, you have a strong foundation to act with integrity in your challenges and responsibilities. When your life is governed by God's standards of fairness and justice, you'll be ready to carry out his purposes for your life, and others will trust and follow you.

Is your life built on a strong foundation of honesty?

Trust in His Strength

Then the LORD asked Moses,
"Who makes a person's mouth?
Who decides whether people speak or
do not speak, hear or do not hear,
see or do not see? Is it not I, the LORD?
Now go! I will be with you as you speak,
and I will instruct you in what to say."

EXODUS 4:11-12

When God asks you to do something, he will give you the ability and the extra resources to get the job done. There are no limits to what God can do in and through you.

When you trust in God's strength instead of your own abilities, he promises to give you power to do things you could never do on your own.

What is God asking you to do for him?

Reach Out in Love

You have heard the law that says,
"Love your neighbor" and hate your enemy.
But I say, love your enemies!
Pray for those who persecute you!
In that way, you will be acting as
true children of your Father in heaven.

MATTHEW 5:43-45

It's human nature to love our friends and hate our enemies. But Jesus gives us a new, divine perspective—the only way to resolve some conflicts is to love and pray for your enemy.

You are maturing as a child of God when it becomes more natural for you to reach out in love to those who are against you.

* * *

Is there someone with whom
you are in conflict? How can
you show love to that person?

Maturing in Godliness

This will continue until we all come to such unity in our faith and knowledge of God's Son that we will be mature in the Lord, measuring up to the full and complete standard of Christ.

EPHESIANS 4:13

Achieving godliness does not mean reaching a flawless imitation of God; rather, it is a process of maturing toward perfection. Godliness means becoming more like God even while falling far short of the goal in this life. But you can look forward to a day when the process of reflecting God's nature will be complete and you will indeed be perfect—when you reach heaven.

If you keep striving to become more like God in your thoughts and actions, he promises that you will one day be perfect, without sin or fault of any kind.

Are you maturing in godliness?
How might this impact the people you lead?

Despite Your Limitations

Each one of you will put to flight a thousand of the enemy, for the LORD your God fights for you, just as he has promised.

JOSHUA 23:10

You can be encouraged by the fact that God fights for you, regardless of the odds against you.

The Bible gives us many examples: God used the young boy David to overcome the giant Goliath; God used Gideon's three hundred soldiers to defeat the countless thousands of Midianite soldiers; and God used the twelve disciples to establish the whole church. You don't have to be above average for God to do great things through you.

Knowing that God works through you despite your limitations is a great encouragement.

What great work is God doing through you? Do you need God's encouragement to accomplish it?

JUNE

Never Become Complacent

I know all the things you do, that you are neither hot nor cold. I wish that you were one or the other! But since you are like lukewarm water, neither hot nor cold, I will spit you out of my mouth!

REVELATION 3:15-16

God detests complacency. Complacency leads to indifference, and indifference leads to idleness. If you stand for nothing, you don't care about anything. You are apathetic about the needs of the people around you and complacent about sin. This makes it difficult to lead because others need to be motivated by seeing your passion and purpose.

Complacency stands in stark contrast to the Father's command to boldly love and care for those around us.

In what area of your life do you tend to become complacent? How does that affect your relationship with God and others?

Exercise Perseverance

*Keep on asking, and you will receive
what you ask for. Keep on seeking, and
you will find. Keep on knocking,
and the door will be opened to you.*

When you practice perseverance in your prayer life, you demonstrate your faith in God—that he is listening, that he cares, and that he will respond.

As you keep praying, ask God to give you a glimpse of what he wants you to learn through the exercise of perseverance.

*How can you develop greater
perseverance in your prayer life?*

Discipline Improves Who You Are

*Joyful are those you discipline, LORD,
those you teach with your instructions.*

PSALM 94:12

No one likes discipline, and no one wants to hear that it is good for you. But the truth is that without discipline, people will do the wrong things and then suffer the consequences.

Effective discipline sets you back on the right path; it should make you thankful to be going the right way once again. And who better to discipline you than your perfect, loving heavenly Father? He knows just how to help you do the right thing and avoid potential disaster.

God promises that when he disciplines you, it is always to improve who you are and how you live.

Where might you need God's discipline in your life? What good could come as a result of his discipline?

The Timing of God

*The LORD is good to those who depend on him,
to those who search for him. So it is good to
wait quietly for salvation from the LORD.*

LAMENTATIONS 3:25-26

Sometimes the Father answers yes to your prayers. Sometimes he says no. Sometimes he wants you to wait. And sometimes you simply have to give your life over to God's control, even when you don't understand his ways.

Rushing ahead may get you what you think is best, but waiting for God's timing will get God's best for you, and that is always better.

How well are you waiting on God?

Stop the Anger

Stop being angry! Turn from your rage!
Do not lose your temper—it only leads to harm.

Anger is often a reaction to your pride being hurt. When you are confronted, rejected, ignored, or don't get your own way, anger acts as a defense mechanism to protect your ego.

Leaders are especially vulnerable to anger because their character and their actions are constantly being evaluated and scrutinized.

It is common to feel angry when someone confronts you about your own sinful actions because you don't want others to think you have done something wrong. But the Bible promises that anger—unless it is righteous anger—will always bring harm.

What kinds of things cause you to get angry?

A New Heaven and Earth

*We are looking forward to the new heavens
and new earth he has promised,
a world filled with God's righteousness.*

2 PETER 3:13

God originally created earth to be heaven—the place where he would live side by side with humankind and walk and talk with them. Sin changed all that. It separated us from God and corrupted the earth. But God's original plan for a heavenly paradise that is a very physical place—with trees and plants, mountains and waterfalls, fruits and vegetables— will still be accomplished someday. The Bible refers to this as the new earth—the place where we will be reunited with God. If you can encourage those you lead to see this present earth as the place God will someday restore and redeem, you can inspire them to better care for it and to work toward redemption in their own life and the lives of others.

*How can the promise of heaven help you
inspire others to work toward restoration?*

Forgiveness

*When you are praying, first forgive anyone
you are holding a grudge against, so that
your Father in heaven will forgive your sins, too.*

MARK 11:25

Leaders must understand that refusing to forgive a person can lead to serious and rather harmful consequences for the offender. It is acceptable, even necessary, to allow people to experience the natural and logical consequences for their mistakes or offenses. But you should not discourage them further by withholding forgiveness.

When you develop an attitude of forgiveness, you display to others your own gratitude for how much God has forgiven you. Your willingness to forgive others depends on your appreciation for how much God has forgiven you.

Who might need your forgiveness today?

A Peaceful Heart

A cheerful heart is good medicine,
but a broken spirit saps a person's strength.

PROVERBS 17:22

A peaceful heart leads to a healthy body;
jealousy is like cancer in the bones.

PROVERBS 14:30

Attitude changes everything. Faith is an attitude of trust that believes the events in your life happen under God's direction—they're not just random circumstances. This allows you to view your life from a perspective of hope rather than defeat.

It allows you to have a positive attitude about your circumstances because you know God will take whatever happens in your life and bring good from it.

Is it time for an attitude check?
Go to God's Word to gain God's perspective.

The Hand of God

Come and see what our God has done, what awesome miracles he performs for people!

PSALM 66:5

God works on behalf of his people in miraculous ways. The daily news is filled with all the terrible things that are happening in the world.

But if you step back for a moment, you can begin to get a glimpse of God's hand quietly working miracles in many people's lives—including yours—every day. His hand is there, even when you don't see it.

Has anything happened in your life or the life of someone you lead that might be from the hand of God?

Listen to Godly Advice

Fools think their own way is right,
but the wise listen to others.

PROVERBS 12:15

The Bible promises that rejecting wise advice will lead to mistakes. Good words and actions are the result of good thoughts and character.

When you spend your time thinking about what is good and right and listening to people who are godly and wise, you will avoid many mistakes.

As a leader, you must be discerning about whom you listen to. Then your decisions will be wise and helpful to others.

Does the advice you get from others help you avoid mistakes, or could it get you into trouble?

Work Together

He makes the whole body fit together perfectly.
As each part does its own special work,
it helps the other parts grow, so that the whole
body is healthy and growing and full of love.

EPHESIANS 4:16

Community is essential for effective leadership. In fact, leadership can be defined in part as "accomplishment through community." Leaders get things done with and through other people.

The Bible gives countless examples of leaders who developed community within large and small groups in order to fulfill God's will. Study God's Word to learn from their example.

In what way can you develop a greater sense of community among the people you lead?

The Call of God

*Now may the God of peace ... equip you with
all you need for doing his will. May he produce
in you, through the power of Jesus Christ,
every good thing that is pleasing to him.*

HEBREWS 13:20-21

You know how frustrating it is to be given an assignment without the resources to accomplish it. But when the heavenly Father calls you to a task, he equips you for it. If you are attuned to hearing his call, you can be sure that he will give you the resources to fulfill his assignment.

He gives you his Word for counsel and direction, special abilities and gifts to use as you pursue the task, and his Holy Spirit to give you strength and guidance along the way. When you tap into everything he has given you, you will accomplish great things for him.

*Are you attuned to God's call? Where
will you get the resources to fulfill it?*

Serving God

Good comes to those who lend money generously and conduct their business fairly.

PSALM 112:5

God gives us advice about business because that's where so many people spend the most productive hours of their day.

Even though you probably can't choose much of what you have to do during the day, you can choose who you are and how you react. That will impact your work far more than you realize.

God promises that your greatest fulfillment will come when you focus on filling needs and serving God as your ultimate bottom line.

What principles are you using to conduct yourself at work?

Letting Go

Then call on me when you are in trouble,
and I will rescue you, and you will give me glory.

PSALM 50:15

The more you try to hold on to and control every situation, the less you hold on to God. But the more you trust God, the more he holds on to you. Letting go does not mean giving up.

Letting go means allowing God to work while you obediently stand and watch. It means watching for God's next move. So if God says stand and watch, then stand and watch him work. And praise him as he works!

Do what you know is right for as long as you can possibly do it, and then trust God's promise to take it from there.

What do you have trouble letting go of?

Strong Convictions

God has given both his promise and his oath.
These two things are unchangeable because
it is impossible for God to lie.
Therefore, we who have fled to him for refuge
can have great confidence as we hold
to the hope that lies before us.

HEBREWS 6:18

Conviction is more than just having a belief; it is a commitment to a belief. What you think, say, and do shows the level of your conviction.

Convictions hold you steady on God's path for your life and help you faithfully live out your belief in God in practical ways. Keep your convictions strong, and your life will be a great story of faith in God.

What convictions most help
you live out your faith?

Positive Words Make an Impact

*If you claim to be religious but don't control
your tongue, you are fooling yourself,
and your religion is worthless.*

JAMES 1:26

Exercising self-control over your words includes discernment in both what you shouldn't say and what you should say. How often do you even take notice of what comes out of your mouth? Ask a friend to help you make a list of the positive and negative words you typically speak.

To stop the negative words, before you say something ask yourself, "Is it true? Is it kind? Is it helpful?" If you can answer yes to these questions, your positive words will have an amazing impact on others.

---

*How can you make sure you have
more positive than negative words
coming from your mouth and heart?*

Peak Performance

How can a ... person stay pure?
By obeying your word.

PSALM 119:9

If you buy a new computer but neglect to read the instruction manual, you'll miss out on many of the functions the machine is capable of doing. You'll be operating with just enough knowledge to perform basic functions.

When it comes to reading the Bible, most of us read just enough to get by. We miss so much of what God's Word has to offer. Study the Bible daily so you can thoroughly understand everything God wants you to know. Then you will be able to live and lead at peak performance.

What can you do to develop the habit
of studying God's Word more regularly?

Perfect Knowledge

*Fear of the LORD is the foundation
of true knowledge,
but fools despise wisdom and discipline.*

PROVERBS 1:7

If you really want to know what is important, what really matters, start with God. After all, God is the Creator of life and has perfect knowledge of how it should work. The Father alone can reveal the true secret to success.

So as you grow in knowledge of your business or other skills, make sure to include the wisdom that comes from the Creator of life. Then you will know not only your work but why your work matters.

———— • ————

*How can you integrate the goal of knowing
your work with the goal of knowing God?*

The Heavenly Norm

*The world would love you as one of its own
if you belonged to it, but you are no longer part
of the world. I chose you to come out of the world,
so it hates you. ... Since they persecuted me,
naturally they will persecute you. And if they
had listened to me, they would listen to you.
They will do all this to you because of me,
for they have rejected the One who sent me.*

JOHN 15:19-21

God's message is countercultural. When you follow his ways—for example, by praying for your enemies or giving away your money to help others—it will not make sense according to today's cultural standards.

As a result, you can expect some ridicule and opposition. But that won't always be the norm. In God's new culture in heaven, goodness and righteousness will be the norm.

———— • ————

Is the way you live each day countercultural?

Where You Truly Belong

What blessings await you when people hate you and exclude you and mock you and curse you as evil because you follow the Son of Man.

LUKE 6:22

Consider your status as an outsider here on earth to be a blessing rather than a curse. You can look forward to receiving God's eternal blessing for the ridicule you endure today.

As a Christian, you do not belong in this world—your real home is in heaven. Other believers are outsiders like you. Their friendship and accountability can encourage you to humbly and faithfully obey God. Then God promises you will reach the place where you truly belong.

Are there other Christians you can turn to when you feel you don't belong?

God's Vision for Your Life

*"My thoughts are nothing like your thoughts,"
says the LORD. "And my ways are far beyond
anything you could imagine. For just as the
heavens are higher than the earth, so my ways
are higher than your ways and my thoughts
higher than your thoughts."*

ISAIAH 55:8-9

You already have some vision about the future. Seeking God's vision breaks your bondage to small ideas that are not worthy of God or representative of God's work in the world. God's vision expands your mind to greater possibilities.

By aligning your vision with God's vision for your life, you will be inspired to pursue your future with purpose and clarity.

Are you seeking God's vision for your life?

Lead with Justice

*Then Peter replied, "I see very clearly that God
shows no favoritism. In every nation he accepts
those who fear him and do what is right."*

ACTS 10:34-35

Leadership is vital for order, productivity, and
teamwork. Problems come when leaders abuse their
authority and act as though their position gives
them superior value. If you fail to see others as equal
in value, injustice and evil will get the upper hand.

Being a child of God outranks any human position or status. To look at yourself as superior to others
is to devalue their worth in God's eyes. To lead with
justice and fairness, you must see everyone as having
equal worth before God.

———— • ————

*What can you do to make sure you see yourself
and your coworkers as equals in God's eyes?*

Serve Others

*May you experience the love of Christ, though
it is too great to understand fully. Then you
will be made complete with all the fullness
of life and power that comes from God.*

EPHESIANS 3:19

Jesus understood that there is something fundamentally fulfilling about living to serve others, and that to live only for yourself leads to emptiness and disappointment. Merely getting rid of the bad within you leaves you empty and open to something even worse.

It is only through serving others that meaning, purpose, and satisfaction are restored. Since God made you for a specific purpose, you will only find true meaning when you fill your soul with him.

What are you trying to fill your heart with?

A Greater Understanding

*Keep on asking, and you will receive what you
ask for. Keep on seeking, and you will find.
Keep on knocking, and the door will be opened
to you. For everyone who asks, receives.
Everyone who seeks, finds. And to everyone
who knocks, the door will be opened.*

MATTHEW 7:7-8

There's more to prayer than just getting an answer to a question or a solution to a problem. God often does more in your heart through your act of praying than he does in actually answering your prayer.

As you persist in talking and listening to God, he promises you will gain greater understanding of yourself, your situation, your motivation, and God's purpose and direction for you and your life.

*How can your prayer life be
a conversation with God?*

New-Found Meaning

*Imitate God, therefore, in everything
you do, because you are his dear children.
Live a life filled with love, following the
example of Christ. ... For once you were full
of darkness, but now you have light from
the Lord. So live as people of light! For this
light within you produces only what
is good and right and true.*

ЕPHESIANS 5:1-2, 8-9

If you try to follow Jesus' example daily, you will never become bored! When your relationship with him grows so that you easily recognize his purpose for you, your life will take on new meaning.

To have this kind of relationship, daily try to follow Jesus' example. Since he was perfect but you can't achieve perfection this side of heaven, you will always be challenged to keep working at it.

---

*What can you do today to
follow Jesus' example?*

Faith That Lasts

So we don't look at the troubles we can see now; rather, we fix our gaze on things that cannot be seen. For the things we see now will soon be gone, but the things we cannot see will last forever.

2 CORINTHIANS 4:18

God promises that the things you can see and touch—the tangible things of this world—won't last. But the things you can't see or touch—faith, heaven, God's supernatural work—will last forever.

Your goal, therefore, is to put your faith in the things you can't see and avoid putting your faith in the here and now. When you begin living with this new perspective, you will see your hurts and troubles as part of this tangible and temporary world, and you will have faith that they won't last. Then your hope and confidence in a world where there will be no hurt or pain will become even stronger and the positive influence you have on others will become greater.

How might God turn your hurt into a blessing for others?

Endure to the End

*Of course, you get no credit for being patient
if you are beaten for doing wrong.
But if you suffer for doing good and
endure it patiently, God is pleased with you.*

Nearly all Christians are persecuted for their faith at some point along life's journey. In many countries, Christians suffer torture and death because of their faith. When you feel like quitting, you are focusing too much on this life, not the life you will live for eternity if you endure.

Endurance in the face of suffering and ridicule is necessary to receive the prize of eternal life, and those who endure have a special place in God's heart and a special place of influence in this life.

*When you feel like quitting your walk of faith,
what can motivate you to keep going?*

The Body of Christ

*God has put all things under the authority
of Christ and has made him head over all
things for the benefit of the church. And
the church is his body; it is made full and
complete by Christ, who fills all
things everywhere with himself.*

EPHESIANS 1:22-23

Even though Satan tries to attack the church, Jesus promises that his body of believers will not be overcome. God will continue to do great things through the church. The people of God are equipped with the resurrection power of Jesus Christ, and they are his representatives to the world.

When you and other believers come together with this vision, you can have confidence that God will be at work through his church. Together you will accomplish more than anyone could imagine.

*What part are you playing in
God's plan for his church?*

Pursue Holiness

Work at living in peace with everyone,
and work at living a holy life,
for those who are not holy will not see the Lord.

HEBREWS 12:14

Living at peace with others is an indicator of the health of your relationship with God. When you live a holy life, you are always trying your best to treat others with the same mercy and unconditional love that God would show to them and that he already has shown to you.

You will stumble at times, but all God asks is that you sincerely try to be more like him each day. The more you understand what God has done to make peace with you, the more you understand the benefits of pursuing holiness and peaceful relationships with others.

———— • ————

How can living a life of holiness help
you live peacefully with others?

Strength of Character

*Endurance develops strength of character,
and character strengthens our confident hope
of salvation. And this hope will not lead
to disappointment.*

ROMANS 5:4-5

Developing character is like developing any other skill. It takes practice to improve it.

Keep practicing what is good and right, and develop qualities such as kindness, generosity, compassion, and honesty.

What you work hardest to attain is what you will learn to value the most.

* * *

*Do you have a plan for
strengthening your character?*

JULY

Glory to God

All glory to God, who is able, through his mighty power at work within us, to accomplish infinitely more than we might ask or think.

EPHESIANS 3:20

In God's unlimited knowledge, he created humans with limitations. He did not do this to discourage you but to help you realize your utter need for him. It is in your weakness that God's strength shines the brightest. When you accomplish something great despite your limitations, it is obvious that God was working through you and he deserves the credit. Jesus says, "What is impossible for people is possible with God" (Luke 18:27).

The next time life makes you aware of your limitations, see it as an opportunity for God's power to overcome your human limitations. Eagerly anticipate how God will work through you to accomplish more than you ever could have dreamed.

Which of your limitations frustrate you most? How can you let God's power work through you in those areas of weakness?

Generosity Promotes Giving

Don't forget to do good and to share with those in need. These are the sacrifices that please God.

HEBREWS 13:16

Generosity is both a spiritual gift and a spiritual discipline. It is an important character trait in God's eyes because it is the opposite of selfishness, which is one of the most destructive sins. Selfishness promotes greed, stinginess, envy, and hard-heartedness—traits that destroy relationships and make poor leaders.

Generosity promotes giving, trust, mercy, and putting the needs of others above your own—traits that build relationships and make good leaders.

How generous are you toward those you lead?

God Is for You

Be strong and courageous, and do the work.
Don't be afraid or discouraged,
for the LORD God, my God, is with you.
He will not fail you or forsake you.
He will see to it that all the work ...
of the LORD is finished correctly.

1 CHRONICLES 28:20

Attitude is important because it affects your thoughts, motives, and actions. As a believer, you can maintain a positive attitude that is based on the fact that the God of the universe created you, loves you, and promises you salvation and eternal life. God is working for you, not against you.

Remind yourself of these truths every day. It will positively affect your attitude, which will positively affect the way you live and lead and serve God.

On a scale from one to ten, how is your attitude?
How can you bring it up a few notches today?

Choose Real Love

*Look, today I am giving you the choice
between a blessing and a curse! You will
be blessed if you obey the commands of the
LORD your God that I am giving you today.
But you will be cursed if you reject the commands
of the LORD your God and turn away from him.*

DEUTERONOMY 11:26-28

It sounds contradictory, but evil exists because God is loving. The Bible teaches that God created human beings with the freedom to choose—either to love and obey him and do what is right, or to disobey him and do what is wrong. God gave us this gift of freedom because without it, there can be no love.

God could have created us so that we could only do good—thus eliminating the possibility of evil—but then we would be robots without the capacity to choose or to love. Only when you have the freedom to choose does love become real.

*With your freedom of choice,
have you chosen God?*

The God of Impossibilities

Jesus looked at them intently and said,
"Humanly speaking, it is impossible.
But with God everything is possible."

MATTHEW 19:26

Too often our own limitations cause us to doubt God's ability to work through us. It's easy to think up reasons for why things can't happen instead of thinking about how they might happen because our almighty God is involved.

The next time you think a promise from God is too impossible to come true, or you are facing a seemingly impossible problem, look at it from God's perspective and ask him to do the impossible! He promises that at the right moment, he can and will do the impossible in you.

What seems impossible to you as
a leader? Have you looked at the
situation from God's perspective?

Get Your Priorities Straight

He causes us to remember his wonderful works.
How gracious and merciful is our LORD!

PSALM 111:4

It is easy to forget about things that aren't important to you, so make sure that God is your top priority. Then you will be more likely to remember how he has worked in your life before and to go to him first when you need help now.

You can keep your focus on the heavenly Father by remembering how he has worked in your past, by telling others what he is doing in your life now, by meditating on his Word to see how he has worked throughout history, and by sharing his blessings with future generations.

When you make these things your priorities, you help yourself and others remember God's work in the past and see his grace and mercy in the present and the future.

Where is God on your priority list?

Reach Your Eternal Goals

Don't store up treasures here on earth, where
moths eat them and rust destroys them,
and where thieves break in and steal.
Store your treasures in heaven,
where moths and rust cannot destroy,
and thieves do not break in and steal.

MATTHEW 6:19-20

There's nothing wrong with a competitive nature. Just make sure you are not competing for the wrong things with the wrong motives. God doesn't guarantee you earthly accomplishments, but he does guarantee you eternal accomplishments and rewards.

Make sure your competitive nature drives you toward eternal goals, which will last forever.

In what areas are you most competitive?
Is that competitive drive motivated
by earthly or eternal rewards?

Do His Work Boldly

I can do everything through Christ,
who gives me strength.

PHILIPPIANS 4:13

Blessed are those who trust in the LORD and
have made the LORD their hope and confidence.

JEREMIAH 17:7

Confidence can either lead to cockiness, which results in pride and boasting, or it can lead to inner assurance, which produces a healthy self-esteem and a sure conviction of where you are going.

The word for *confidence* in the Bible is also translated as *boldness*. With Christ by your side, you can boldly set forth to do his work, confident that you can do anything within his will.

How confident are you that God
can and will work through you
to accomplish good things?

Point Others to God

*Jesus spoke to the people once more and said,
"I am the light of the world. If you follow me,
you won't have to walk in darkness,
because you will have the light that leads to life."*

JOHN 8:12

Spiritual leaders have a profound impact on how people view God and whether they will walk with him or not.

Make sure you are a leader whose words and actions point others to an accurate picture of God and challenge them to raise their standards in obeying and serving him.

———————

*How well can others see God
when they are following you?*

Seek Good Advice

Plans go wrong for lack of advice;
many advisers bring success.

PROVERBS 15:22

Leaders continually face complex problems that seem to involve endless variables and options. Wise leaders seek the counsel and expertise of others. Fools often try to go it alone because they are too proud or ignorant to understand the risks.

God promises that the more you seek advice, the more successful your plans will be.

Whom can you go to for advice about
a problem you're currently dealing with?

Neighborly Love in Action

A second [commandment] is equally important: "Love your neighbor as yourself."

MATTHEW 22:39

Jesus taught that loving your neighbor as yourself is the second greatest commandment. Why? Because God knows that human instinct is to take care of yourself first.

But if you can train yourself to give equal priority to meeting the needs of others as well as your own needs, then you will know what love is all about.

If you truly love others the way God intended, you will naturally carry out God's other instructions for service. Love directed inward has nowhere to go; love directed outward can change the world one person at a time.

How well are you loving your neighbors or coworkers?

You Are Useful

Even in old age they will still produce fruit;
they will remain vital and green.
They will declare, "The LORD is just!
He is my rock! There is no evil in him!"

PSALM 92:14-15

The Bible is filled with stories of older people whom God used. Even if your physical abilities are limited, you can serve God in valuable ways, such as in the ministries of prayer and encouragement. Older people have seen God's hand at work in their lives over many years.

Look at it as a privilege to be able to share this perspective with those who are younger, strengthening their faith with evidence of God's faithfulness to you. No matter how old you are, you can never outlive your usefulness to God!

* * *

What spiritual encouragement can
you share with those who are younger
than you? Or what can you learn
from those who are older than you?

A Holy Outlook

Our High Priest offered himself to God as a single sacrifice for sins. ... By that one offering he forever made perfect those who are being made holy.

HEBREWS 10:12-14

Because of your sins, it is not possible to be holy on your own. But when you ask God's Holy Spirit to control your thoughts and actions, you have taken the first important step toward becoming more holy.

The word *holy* comes from the root word that means "to be separate" or "to be set apart." As such, holiness includes not only moral integrity but also your entire outlook on life as you realize that you are in the world but not of it.

God promises to help you break free from the sinful attractions of this world so that you can live for him and really make a difference.

Do you have a holy outlook on life?

Pursue Excellence

Work willingly at whatever you do,
as though you were working for the Lord
rather than for people.
Remember that the Lord will
give you an inheritance as your reward,
and that the Master you are serving is Christ.

COLOSSIANS 3:23-24

Pursuing excellence helps others experience excellence, giving them a glimpse of God and inspiring them to pursue excellence themselves.

God initiated excellence in the beauty of his creation, and you are called to perpetuate it. You can do this first by striving to accomplish God's purpose in your life to the best of your ability. Your life displays excellence when you consistently strive to model God's perfect character as you go about the work he has called you to do. You'll never be perfect in this life, but as you work toward that goal, you will model excellence to those around you.

In what area can you pursue excellence today?

Work for Justice

The righteous LORD loves justice.
The virtuous will see his face.

PSALM 11:7

Leaders cannot ignore it when others are being treated unjustly. Otherwise they are in danger of becoming callous toward the needs of others, or even becoming corrupt.

Be an advocate for justice, and your heart will move you to be a champion of those who need your help to receive fair treatment.

God promises that those who work for justice will experience his presence in powerful ways.

Are you moved when you
see injustice around you?

Be Discerning

Fear of the LORD is the foundation of wisdom.
Knowledge of the Holy One results
in good judgment.

PROVERBS 9:10

Discernment is a stepping-stone on the path to wisdom. It enables you to see behind the facades that mask God's truth.

The devil is the father of lies, but God is the source of all truth, and he promises to give you discernment when you seek it.

Have you made the connection
between your knowledge of God
and your level of discernment?

In His Embrace

*I know all the things you do, and I have opened
a door for you that no one can close.
You have little strength,
yet you obeyed my word and did not deny me.*

REVELATION 3:8

God promises he won't abandon you but will help you through your impossible situations. You should do what you can to the best of your ability, but then let God take it from there.

If God wants you to accomplish a task, he will enable you to do it. When you live by God's principles, you remain in the embrace of his helping arms.

Do you believe God will do the impossible for you? All he's looking for is faith and obedience.

A Life of Goodness

*You are controlled by the Spirit if you have
the Spirit of God living in you.*

ROMANS 8:9

*We will speak the truth in love,
growing in every way more and more like Christ,
who is the head of his body, the church.*

EPHESIANS 4:15

To be like Christ means to be controlled by the Holy Spirit and to do good things motivated by your love for God and others.

Being like Christ runs deeper than nice actions; it reflects a heart of integrity. If you want to be a good person, you have to allow God to change you deep down inside.

As you become more like Jesus, your actions will reflect his goodness. As he takes control of your heart, you will begin to live a life of goodness.

Are you becoming more and more like Christ?

God's Definition of Success

Now all glory to God, who is able to keep you from falling away and will bring you with great joy into his glorious presence without a single fault.

JUDE 1:24

Learn to live by God's definition of failure and success. The world defines success as an abundance of achievements and possessions, and failure as a lack of achievements and possessions.

God defines success as obedience to him, which results in love, godly character, right living, salvation, and eternal life in heaven. God defines failure as rejecting him. Live by God's definition of success, and your failures will only be temporary.

———— • ————

What can you do today to focus on God's definition of success?

Model Truth

*Yes, what joy for those whose record
the LORD has cleared of guilt,
whose lives are lived in complete honesty!*

PSALM 32:2

Deception, the opposite of truth, breaks the bond of trust that is so necessary in human relationships. Without trust, relationships deteriorate. Since the Father created us for relationship, both with others and with himself, it is easy to understand why he hates deception.

God is truth; deception is lies. The good news is that because God is truth, he will never deceive you. You can count on him and believe everything he says. The more you model truth and honesty, the stronger your relationships will be.

*What priority do you place on telling
the truth in your relationships?*

Realize God's Great Love

The joy of the LORD is your strength!

NEHEMIAH 8:10

Joy springs from God's love, and God's love does not depend on your circumstances or performance.

When you realize just how great God's love for you really is, you will be less vulnerable to the depression and despair that can come from problems and disappointments.

Where do you find joy?

Experiencing Deep Joy

*If you look carefully into the perfect law that
sets you free, and if you do what it says and
don't forget what you heard, then God
will bless you for doing it.*

JAMES 1:25

The Bible promises that if you obey the Father by obeying the truths and principles in his Word, he will bless you with a quality of life you would never have otherwise. This quality of life is not measured by material things you might own or want but by the peace of mind and the deep joy with which you can live every day.

Obedience to God ensures that you will never be deprived of your heavenly future, your relationship with God, or your love for others.

*How can obedience be something you
want to do rather than have to do?
How might this affect the people you lead?*

Lying Destroys Trust

The Scriptures say, "If you want to enjoy life and see many happy days, keep your tongue from speaking evil and your lips from telling lies."

1 PETER 3:10

Lying is deceiving someone. It can be blatant or it can be subtle. Lying is selfish and self-serving, for it always attempts to hide and deceive, to take what you have not earned, or to leave an impression you do not deserve.

To fall short of truth, in any way, is to lie. You cannot follow the God of truth while you consistently tell lies—even "little white lies."

Lying destroys trust, and trust is the key to strong relationships. That is why the Bible promises that a happy life is an honest life.

How can you commit to being honest today?

Hope in the Lord

*Joyful are those who have the God
of Israel as their helper,
whose hope is in the LORD their God.*

PSALM 146:5

Throughout the Bible, you find a simple but profound principle: Obeying the heavenly Father brings blessings, and disobeying him brings misfortune. Don't think of blessings only in terms of material possessions. The greatest blessings are far more valuable than money or things. They come in the form of joy, family and friends, relationships, a well-managed team of coworkers, peace of mind, spiritual gifts, and the confidence of eternal life.

A life focused on God brings joy to God and blessings to you. The more you trust and obey God, the more you will experience the blessings he gives.

*What blessings have you experienced
from obeying God? How can you
pursue more of those blessings today?*

Develop Your Gentleness

*Come to me, all of you who are weary and
carry heavy burdens, and I will give you rest.
Take my yoke upon you. Let me teach you,
because I am humble and gentle at heart,
and you will find rest for your souls.*

MATTHEW 11:28-29

In a world full of violence, the concept of gentleness
is a welcome one. There is peace in the life of gentle
people that soothes those around them. Business-
people appreciate a gentle spirit in the office.

Church meetings run more smoothly when a spirit
of gentleness is present. Jesus was gentle. Did this rob
him of authority? No. Good leaders can be gentle
because their power is under control.

The Bible calls you to be gentle in your dealings
with others, not only because it is kind and right but
because it promotes peace and gets results.

How can you work on developing gentleness?

Available for His Purpose

Don't copy the behavior and customs of this world, but let God transform you into a new person by changing the way you think. Then you will learn to know God's will for you, which is good and pleasing and perfect.

ROMANS 12:1-2

Are you busier than ever? At the end of another frantic day, do you slump into your easy chair and say to yourself, *So what?* Does your life seem to lack a purpose worthy of one who is created in God's image?

God does have a purpose for you. When you give yourself to God, he promises to make known his purpose for you as you make yourself available to him.

———————

Do you think about God only at the end of your day, after your work is done? Or do you remember him at the beginning of your day, when you can receive his guidance for the work ahead?

Help in Times of Need

Because of Christ and our faith in him,
we can now come boldly and confidently
into God's presence.

EPHESIANS 3:12

Let us come boldly to the throne of our
gracious God. There we will receive his mercy,
and we will find grace to help us
when we need it most.

HEBREWS 4:16

The assurance of God's love gives you courage to come to him with any problem, struggle, or concern.

Your prayers are never interruptions to the Lord but rather the means to open the floodgates of God's mercy and grace. God meets you where you most need him.

Are you looking for the assurance of God's love?

Sound Investments

*Owe nothing to anyone—except for your obligation
to love one another. If you love your neighbor,
you will fulfill the requirements of God's law.*

ROMANS 13:8

The best investments with the highest rewards are your relationships. When you have so much to do every day, it's easy to forget how important it is to invest in people. But it is by investing in others that you increase your eternal inheritance.

Love the people God has placed in your community. Find practical ways to be a good leader and a loving neighbor by helping those in need.

---

*What investments have you made
lately that will pay off for eternity?*

A Job Well Done

Pay careful attention to your own work, for then you will get the satisfaction of a job well done, and you won't need to compare yourself to anyone else. For we are each responsible for our own conduct.

GALATIANS 6:4-5

You will find great satisfaction in doing your work well. On the other hand, avoiding your responsibilities will leave you feeling guilty and will greatly lower your self-esteem.

There is no need to compare yourself to others when you are satisfied with your work because you are doing what God wants you to do.

Do you focus more on what others are doing or on what you are doing for God?

Slow Down

This is what the Sovereign LORD, the Holy One of Israel, says: "Only in returning to me and resting in me will you be saved. In quietness and confidence is your strength."

ISAIAH 30:15

It is crucial to pause from time to time to renew and restore yourself to a closer fellowship with God. When you spend longer stretches of quiet time with him, you can tap into his strength and hear his voice more clearly. Maybe you find it difficult to stop and be quiet. You mistakenly believe that productivity requires constant activity.

But sometimes you need to slow down in order to speed up—to stop awhile to let your body, mind, and spirit recover and to rediscover your purpose. When you take time to be quiet, you will be more energized and productive because you will have a clearer sense of what God wants you to do.

When was the last time you were quiet before God for an extended period of time?

Study the Scriptures

*All Scripture is inspired by God and is useful
to teach us what is true and to make us realize
what is wrong in our lives. It corrects us when
we are wrong and teaches us to do what is right.*

2 TIMOTHY 3:16

If someone tries to convince you to do something that contradicts the Bible, you can be assured it is definitely wrong.

If you know Scripture well enough, you will be able to discern whether or not something is true.

———— • ————

*Will you commit yourself to studying Scripture
so you can easily recognize the truth?*

AUGUST

Doors of Opportunity

Pharaoh said to Joseph, "Since God has revealed the meaning of the dreams to you, clearly no one else is as intelligent or wise as you are. You will be in charge of my court, and all my people will take orders from you. Only I, sitting on my throne, will have a rank higher than yours."

GENESIS 41:39-40

Responsibility is one of the keys to opening doors of opportunity. How you handle each of your responsibilities, big or small, determines whether or not you will be trusted with more.

When Joseph was unjustly imprisoned, he could have become bitter and done nothing. Instead, he seized every opportunity he could, earned others' trust because of his responsibility, and eventually rose to great prominence in Egypt. When you handle even your minor, day-to-day responsibilities well, you can expect greater opportunities.

How responsible are you in handling every opportunity, both big and small?

Satisfaction in Eternity

*Just as Death and Destruction are never satisfied,
so human desire is never satisfied.*

PROVERBS 27:20

Just as drinking saltwater actually makes you thirstier, the Bible promises that getting more of something actually makes you less satisfied. When you get what you want, you will still want more of it. The perpetual quest to satisfy your desires leaves a growing, consuming emptiness that is never filled.

The desire to be satisfied with earthly things (money, achievements) perpetuates a cycle of dissatisfaction, a never-ending drive for just one more thing. As a result, you are never satisfied with what you have.

The sooner you understand this principle, the sooner you can begin to find true satisfaction by letting go of the temporary and seeking after the eternal.

---

*Are you dissatisfied with what life has to offer?
What does God offer that truly satisfies?*

Troubles Help You Grow

We can rejoice, too, when we run into problems and trials, for we know that they help us develop endurance.

Troubles test your faith. They can strengthen your resolve or break you. It all depends on your attitude. If you see your problems as stepping-stones to something greater, then you can move ahead with anticipation for what you will become—a person of strong character who can handle any obstacle.

If you see your problems as insurmountable barriers, you will get discouraged, give up, and turn back, preventing yourself from becoming more than you are now. God promises that problems and troubles can help you grow. Will you allow him to work that growth in you?

Are you able to welcome the growth that can come from your troubles?

Return to Him

*Don't tear your clothing in your grief, but tear
your hearts instead. Return to the LORD your God,
for he is merciful and compassionate, slow
to get angry and filled with unfailing love.
He is eager to relent and not punish.*

JOEL 2:13

When you have sinned and let others down or when you are humiliated by your own actions, it can feel as if God has turned his back on you, that he is eager to punish you.

Despite your sin, God waits eagerly and patiently for you to return to him. He longs to respond to you in love and forgiveness, showing his mercy and kindness to restore you so you can be even more productive and effective in serving him.

How has God been patient with you?

Use What You Have Well

Yes, each of us will give a personal account to God.

ROMANS 14:12

The goal of stewardship is to make the best possible use of what you have in order to make the greatest possible impact on others so that God's work can move forward as efficiently and effectively as possible. You are ultimately accountable to God for how you use your gifts and opportunities, whether for yourself or for the benefit of others.

God entrusts you with certain resources and abilities and then expects you to maximize them through wise and godly stewardship. He promises to reward you if you use well what God has entrusted to you.

Are you a good steward of the resources and abilities God has given you?

Obedience Sparks Passion

So we must listen very carefully to the truth we have heard, or we may drift away from it.

HEBREWS 2:1

When apathy settles in, it means passion and purpose are gone. If you are apathetic about something, you don't care much about it. For example, if you are apathetic toward the standards of living found in God's Word, your motivation to obey him will fade, and your God-given talents and gifts will be wasted.

One antidote for apathy is serving others—put your faith into action even if you don't feel motivated. The simple act of obedience to God often sparks spiritual passion and motivation.

Have you drifted away from leading according to the truths of God's Word? How can you renew your spiritual passion?

Saved by Grace

*God saved you by his grace when you believed.
And you can't take credit for this;
it is a gift from God. Salvation is not a reward
for the good things we have done,
so none of us can boast about it.*

EPHESIANS 2:8-9

God's ultimate act of grace is an example of how you are to extend grace to others. Be quick to forgive, hasty to extend kindness, generous in love—even when others don't deserve it.

One of the most priceless gifts anyone can receive is the gift of grace. Grace is always undeserved and unexpected yet so appreciated. When you extend grace to someone, you give them the same wonderful gift God has given to you so many times.

Can you give someone the gift of grace today?

A Change of Heart

Who may worship in your sanctuary, LORD?
Who may enter your presence on your holy hill?
Those who lead blameless lives and do what is
right, speaking the truth from sincere hearts.
Those who refuse to gossip or harm their
neighbors or speak evil of their friends.

PSALM 15:1-3

Your words show what kind of person you are. Criticism, gossip, flattery, lying, and profanity are not only word problems, they are heart problems as well.

Simply trying to control your words isn't enough. First you need a change of heart; then good, kind, and healing words will follow.

———— • ————

What do your words say about
the condition of your heart?

Part of His Plans

You can make many plans,
but the LORD's purpose will prevail.

PROVERBS 19:21

It is not that planning is futile. Rather, the promise for today gives you the good news that your plans cannot mess up God's plans.

His plans will ultimately prevail. And if you are following him, you are part of his good plans!

———— • ————

Are your plans carrying out God's plans,
or is God working his will despite your plans?

Rejoice Always

Dear brothers and sisters, when troubles come your way, consider it an opportunity for great joy. For you know that when your faith is tested, your endurance has a chance to grow.

JAMES 1:2-3

You can glorify the heavenly Father even in the most difficult of circumstances.

When you do, two wonderful things happen: You learn to rely on God instead of yourself, and others are blessed by seeing your faith and hope in action.

What difficult circumstances are you experiencing right now? How might God use them for good?

A Life of Integrity

If you keep yourself pure, you will be a special utensil for honorable use. Your life will be clean, and you will be ready for the Master to use you for every good work.

2 TIMOTHY 2:21

If you want to be used by God, you must commit yourself to a life of integrity. Integrity begins with the small decisions you make and actions you take when no one else is watching.

It blossoms into the guiding principle of your life and relationships when you achieve consistency between your beliefs and behavior.

Then when God calls you to a special task, you will be faithful and dependable in handling it.

What steps are you taking to develop the kind of integrity God desires for putting you to good use?

Right Things the Right Way

Because the Sovereign LORD helps me,
I will not be disgraced. Therefore,
I have set my face like a stone,
determined to do his will.
And I know that I will not be put to shame.

ISAIAH 50:7

You can determine that something is the right thing to do when:

(1) you are certain it would please God.

(2) it does not contradict God's Word.

(3) it does not require improper methods (like deception) to accomplish it.

If these requirements are met, then move ahead with confidence. Do the right thing the right way, and you will not regret your decision.

How can you know that you
are making good decisions?

Stand Strong

When the Spirit of truth comes,
he will guide you into all truth.

JOHN 16:13

For every child of God defeats this evil world,
and we achieve this victory through our faith.

1 JOHN 5:4

When you believe the truths taught in God's Word and live by them, you will have the upper hand in any battle against evil.

When you are loyal to God and ask for his help, he will give you discernment to help protect you from Satan and his demons, which are fighting even now for your soul. The Word of God and the power of the Holy Spirit are powerful resources that can overpower any enemy.

Stand strong and confident in the truth, and you can be certain that God will fight your battles and give you the victory.

Are you confident of eternal victory
because of who is fighting for you?

Courage to Face Change

*We know that God causes everything
to work together for the good
of those who love God and are called
according to his purpose for them.*

ROMANS 8:28

Change is part of God's plan for you. What you are headed toward will give you joy and satisfaction beyond your expectations.

That doesn't mean it will be easy, but it will be fulfilling because God has called you there.

Remember that the greatest advances in life come through change.

Where do you find the courage to face change?

Rewarded Accordingly

*So whether we are here in this body or away
from this body, our goal is to please him.
For we must all stand before Christ to be judged.
We will each receive whatever we deserve for
the good or evil we have done in this earthly body.*

2 CORINTHIANS 5:9-10

The knowledge that one day we must stand before the Lord Jesus Christ to account for everything we have done should motivate us to avoid what is wrong and worthless.

For followers of Christ, there is no judgment of salvation—he has already forgiven us—but there is judgment of evaluation, when our good works will be assessed. We will be rewarded according to our faithfulness or lack thereof.

What motivates you to do good?

Avoid Sin

Come close to God, and God will come close to you.
Wash your hands, you sinners;
purify your hearts, for your loyalty is divided
between God and the world.

JAMES 4:8

Avoiding some things will harm you, but avoiding other things will help you. The key is understanding the difference. Staying away from metal during an electrical storm can save your life. But the strong metal frame of a car can save your life in an accident.

In matters of faith, you should try to avoid sin at all costs because it can be deadly. But avoiding God's divine guidance can be just as deadly.

Instead of avoiding God, approach him. He promises that you will develop a relationship with him and discover the difference between the things you should and should not avoid.

———— • ————

Have you been avoiding sin or avoiding God?

A Helping Hand

Do not withhold good from those who deserve it when it's in your power to help them.

PROVERBS 3:27

We often applaud those with a strong, independent spirit, but no one can really survive alone. That's why God created us to be in relationship with other people. Part of being in relationship is giving and receiving help. We need help to get our work done. We need help to develop our skills.

We need help to think through problems. We need help to say, "I'm sorry." God wants to help us too. He is the ultimate helper, for he is wiser, stronger, and more loving than any human being. Cultivate the habit of seeking help from God and others, and offer help to those in need. Then you will become the kind of person God created you to be.

Where could you use more help?
Where could you help others more?

Address Your Weak Spots

Do not let sin control the way you live;
do not give in to sinful desires.

ROMANS 6:12

Your weaknesses are the areas you refuse to give over to God, the areas in which you compromise your convictions for a few moments of pleasure. They are the joints in your spiritual armor at which the enemy takes aim.

You must understand your weaknesses so you can arm yourself against Satan's attacks. It would be a disaster to discover your weak spots in the heat of the battle; you must discover them before the fighting can even begin.

With God's help and a strategy to protect your points of vulnerability, you will be prepared for any of the enemy's attacks.

———— • ————

Are you aware of your weak spots, where
Satan will attack you with temptations?

Take a Stand for Christ

*So if you are suffering in a manner that
pleases God, keep on doing what is right,
and trust your lives to the God who created you,
for he will never fail you.*

1 PETER 4:19

Sometimes you may feel all alone when you take a stand for Christ.

Take comfort in knowing that there are others who are equally committed to God.

God sees your loneliness, is there beside you, and will reward your unfailing commitment to him.

———•———

*Do you have the support of other leaders
who are committed to faithfully serving God?*

A Discerning Ear

Your promise revives me;
it comforts me in all my troubles.

PSALM 119:50

Just as a piano is tuned using a standard tuning fork, so you can only get in tune with God by comparing yourself to the unchanging standards for living found in the Bible. As God communicates to you through his Word, you will begin to hear or discern just what he wants of you.

As your spiritual hearing is fine-tuned, you will become a better listener, better able to hear God when he calls you to a certain task that he has reserved just for you.

Would God say that you are a good listener?

Celebrate with Others

If you are bitterly jealous and there is selfish
ambition in your heart, don't cover up the
truth with boasting and lying. For jealousy and
selfishness are not God's kind of wisdom.
Such things are earthly, unspiritual, and demonic.
For wherever there is jealousy and selfish ambition,
there you will find disorder and evil of every kind.

JAMES 3:14-16

Jealousy is desiring what you don't have. It can lead to possessiveness and fear of losing what you do have. Leaders can be crippled by jealousy, driving away their greatest supporters.

Wise leaders learn to celebrate with others the good things they have been given. That is how you can win the loyalty of those you lead.

———— • ————

How might jealousy be hindering your leadership?

Godly Ambition

[Jesus] said, "If any of you wants to be my follower,
you must turn from your selfish ways,
take up your cross, and follow me.
If you try to hang on to your life, you will lose it.
But if you give up your life for my sake and
for the sake of the Good News, you will save it.
And what do you benefit if you gain
the whole world but lose your own soul?"

MARK 8:34-36

There's a difference between wanting to be a part of God's great work and wanting personal greatness through God's work. Human ambition can fool you into striving to gain everything you desire in this world at the cost of losing your reward in heaven.

But God promises that the ambition to be a part of his great work will help you discover meaning in your life as well as give you eternal life with him and heavenly rewards.

What is the source of your ambition?

Seek Support

Two people are better off than one,
for they can help each other succeed.
If one person falls, the other can reach out
and help. But someone who falls alone is
in real trouble. ... A person standing alone can
be attacked and defeated, but two can stand
back-to-back and conquer. Three are even better,
for a triple-braided cord is not easily broken.

ECCLESIASTES 4:9-12

Leaders are sometimes tempted to be lone rangers. Sometimes they feel this is necessary, but other times it's because they simply don't want to be bothered with the complexities and demands of involving others in their work. But the leader who acts alone is vulnerable in many ways.

Wise leaders who seek advice and maintain accountability will find greater support and wisdom and will make better decisions.

Should you be involving other
people to help you lead?

Build a Support System

*Confess your sins to each other and pray for
each other so that you may be healed.*

JAMES 5:16

It can be healing to confess your sin to another person, especially if he or she is committed to praying for you, encouraging you, and supporting you as you seek restoration.

It is especially important to confess sins to the people you have wronged. As a leader, it is essential to build this kind of support system around you to keep you spiritually healthy and help you stand strong against temptation.

*Are you willing to find healing
through confession and forgiveness?*

Love God Whole-Heartedly

"My thoughts are nothing like your thoughts,"
says the LORD. "And my ways are far beyond
anything you could imagine."

ISAIAH 55:8

Sometimes it seems as if God has unrealistic expectations of us. How can we possibly obey all his commands? How can we love according to his standards?

God understands that humanly speaking, these expectations are impossible to fulfill, but with his help they become possible. God's greatest expectation is not that you live a perfect life but that you love him with your whole heart.

Understand that God doesn't expect you to be perfect but rather applauds you when you sincerely try to follow him. Then you will no longer see him as a strict taskmaster but as a loving encourager.

Do you have any faulty expectations of God?

Blessings to Bless Others

*All praise to God, the Father of our Lord
Jesus Christ, who has blessed us with every
spiritual blessing in the heavenly realms
because we are united with Christ.*

EPHESIANS 1:3

If you want God's blessings just so you can live an easier, more comfortable life, then you don't understand the nature of God's blessings.

When you belong to Christ, all that you are and all that you have is a gift from him, to be used by him to bless others.

When you truly desire to serve God, God promises you an abundance of blessings to be used to refresh others.

*How are you using the blessings
God has given you to bless others?*

A Heart of Compassion

*When you are harvesting your crops and forget
to bring in a bundle of grain from your field,
don't go back to get it. Leave it for the foreigners,
orphans, and widows. Then the LORD your God
will bless you in all you do.*

DEUTERONOMY 24:19

Throughout the Bible, God commands his people to treat the poor with compassion and generosity. Today, the powerless and poverty-stricken are often looked upon as incompetent and lazy, but in reality, many are victims of oppression and circumstance.

While not many of us harvest fields, we do have a God-given responsibility to share from our abundance to meet the needs of the poor and less fortunate—in our world, in our local community, in our church, and even in our workplace. God promises that your compassion will not go unnoticed.

Are you developing a heart of compassion?

The Paradox of Peace

God blesses those who work for peace,
for they will be called the children of God.

MATTHEW 5:9

Peace is accomplished through the power of love, not the love of power. Followers of Christ know better than to take matters of law and justice into their own hands. They know that fighting according to the world's ways brings even greater problems.

Instead, practice the paradox of peace—bless your enemy, give when threatened, and feed those who would take your food.

This principle unleashes God's power in the situation. Only he can solve conflict that from a human standpoint cannot be solved.

How can you practice the
paradox of peace today?

Free-Flowing Love

*As a result of your ministry, they will give glory
to God. For your generosity to them and to
all believers will prove that you are obedient
to the Good News of Christ. And they will pray
for you with deep affection because of the
overflowing grace God has given to you.*

2 CORINTHIANS 9:13-14

As a river flows freely through an unblocked channel, so God's grace and blessing flow through you when you follow his ways.

When you obey God, your life becomes an open channel through which his love and mercy can flow to others.

*Is God's love and mercy flowing freely
through you to the people around you?*

Finding Purpose

Our great desire is that you will keep on loving others as long as life lasts, in order to make certain that what you hope for will come true. Then you will not become spiritually dull and indifferent. Instead, you will follow the example of those who are going to inherit God's promises because of their faith and endurance.

HEBREWS 6:11-12

The antidote to boredom is finding something purposeful and significant to do. God has a purpose for you. Find that purpose, and you will never be bored! Try volunteering to help in a ministry in your local church, or find a hobby such as music, crafts, or sports that helps you develop a skill. Then you will look forward to each day.

A spiritual fire will ignite in your heart, and people will be attracted to your enthusiasm and passion for living.

Are you bored with life? How can you find God's purpose for you?

Study Scripture for Guidance

If you need wisdom, ask our generous God, and he will give it to you. He will not rebuke you for asking.

JAMES 1:5

Have you ever asked God for a sign or a miracle so that his guidance will be crystal clear? Although God sometimes works this way, usually he does not. Today, God's greatest means of guidance is his Word. If you want more guidance, study the Bible.

God wrote it and gave it to you for exactly that reason—to serve as a guidebook for getting through life. But he also wants you to have faith, to trust him every step of the way. So read the Bible, ask God what to do next, and then take small steps of faith each day. God promises he will lead you in the right direction.

As you read God's Word today, what do you think God is guiding you to do?

SEPTEMBER

The Right Motives

Pay careful attention to your own work, for then you will get the satisfaction of a job well done, and you won't need to compare yourself to anyone else.

GALATIANS 6:4

We often get stressed out when we take on activities and responsibilities for the wrong reasons.

As you consider upcoming involvements, ask the heavenly Father to help you do things with the right motives and to reveal any area in which your motives are less than pure.

As God guides you, you will begin to know which activities you should do and which ones you should say no to. When you say yes with the right motives, you will work with a passion and purpose that will give you great satisfaction and fulfillment.

Are you saying yes with the right motives?

Overcome Evil with Good

*Don't let evil conquer you,
but conquer evil by doing good.*

ROMANS 12:21

As a follower of Christ, you are part of the church, the people of God. God promises that one day the church will overcome the kingdom of darkness and win the ultimate victory.

Until then, you have work to do and battles to fight against the forces of evil. You must not be only on the defensive, biding your time until victory is won. Take the offensive, and fight to overcome evil with good.

---

*What is God calling you to do now
as part of the battle against evil?*

The Right Kind of Nourishment

Those who drink the water I give will never be thirsty again. It becomes a fresh, bubbling spring within them, giving them eternal life.

JOHN 4:14

Do you ever try to meet your deepest needs in ways that just don't satisfy? Sometimes when you're hungry, the worst thing you can do is eat the wrong thing. If you haven't eaten in a while and you quickly gobble down a few doughnuts, you'll be satisfied for a few minutes until your body experiences the crash after the sugar high.

The same principle applies to satisfying the hungry soul. Fill it with only fun, pleasure, or sin, and you'll always be craving more; you'll never get enough. Your soul will get the shakes. Without taking spiritual nourishment from God, you will never feel satisfied.

Are you feeding your soul the right kind of nourishment?

Desiring God

*If you look for me wholeheartedly,
you will find me.*

JEREMIAH 29:13

Desires are good and healthy when they are directed toward that which is good and right and God honoring. The same basic desire can be right or wrong, depending upon your motives and the object of your desire. For example, the desire to love someone is healthy and right when it is directed toward your spouse in marriage.

But when that same desire is directed toward someone who is not your spouse, it is adultery. The desire to lead an organization is healthy if your motive is to serve others, but it is unhealthy and wrong if your motive is to gain power or control over others. Your greatest desire must be for a relationship with God, which will influence all your other desires.

*Is your greatest desire to know
and love God more each day?*

A Higher Standard

Dear brothers and sisters, not many of you should become teachers in the church, for we who teach will be judged more strictly.

JAMES 3:1

This is a promise with a warning rather than a blessing. Leaders sometimes make the mistake of thinking they are above the rules, exempted from the standards that apply to everyone else. Consequently, they are more vulnerable to pride and temptation.

When leaders give in to this kind of thinking, they lose credibility with others. They put both their work and their relationships in jeopardy. God holds leaders to a higher standard because of their position of influence over others.

What are some of the areas in which God is holding you to a higher standard?

Gradually Purer

Who may climb the mountain of the LORD?
Who may stand in his holy place?
Only those whose hands and hearts are pure,
who ... never tell lies.
They will receive the LORD's blessing and have
a right relationship with God their savior.

PSALM 24:3-5

Integrity is essential to God-honoring leadership. Just as pure gold is the result of a refining process that purifies the metal and tests it with fire, a life of integrity is the result of a refining process in which you are tested daily to see how pure you are.

If God sees that your thoughts and actions are becoming increasingly pure through this testing, then your character is becoming more like his, and you are gradually gaining integrity.

Is your character becoming more like
God's or less like God's each day?

Productive Service

Yes, I am the vine; you are the branches.
Those who remain in me, and I in them,
will produce much fruit. For apart from me
you can do nothing. ... You didn't choose me.
I chose you. I appointed you to go and produce
lasting fruit, so that the Father will give you
whatever you ask for, using my name.

JOHN 15:5, 16

God promises that commitment to him leads to productive service. You can be assured of this because the Father chose you and appointed you to serve him and work for him in a unique way.

When you're committed to him, your work will be productive in ways that really matter. Be committed to him so that you can accomplish the many things he created you to do.

How might greater commitment to
God make you more productive?

Give and You Will Receive

Give, and you will receive. Your gift will return to you in full—pressed down, shaken together to make room for more, running over, and poured into your lap. The amount you give will determine the amount you get back.

LUKE 6:38

Giving is sharing something you own—possessions, time, talents—with someone else. In a deeper sense, giving is sharing something of yourself. Giving originates with the God who gives more blessings to his people than they deserve or expect. He gives the gift of life, the gift of love, the gift of salvation, the gift of eternity in heaven—all priceless gifts.

God also gives us spiritual gifts that we should use to serve each other. The Bible promises that the more we give, the more we will receive—not necessarily in material possessions, but in spiritual and eternal rewards.

How can you develop a bigger heart for giving?

Healed and Restored

The sacrifice you desire is a broken spirit.
You will not reject a broken and
repentant heart, O God.

PSALM 51:17

When you fall as a leader, you must fall to your knees to be restored to God. When you're confronted by your failure or sin, don't run from God. Don't make excuses or give up in despair. Instead, acknowledge your need for God's help.

He will draw close to you when you are broken because of sin in your life. When you turn to God in brokenness over sin, he promises to begin the process of healing and restoration.

———— • ————

Do you need healing and restoration in
your relationship with God or someone else?

Hope for Heaven

*When the Great Shepherd appears, you will
receive a crown of never-ending glory and honor.
In his kindness God called you to share in his
eternal glory by means of Christ Jesus.
So after you have suffered a little while,
he will restore, support, and strengthen you,
and he will place you on a firm foundation.*

1 PETER 5:4, 10

As a heaven-bound follower of Jesus, you need to put heaven and earth in proper perspective. Here on earth, you will live for a hundred years or less. In heaven, a hundred *million* years is just the beginning!

Yet God has determined that how you live during your short time on earth will prepare you for heaven. This gives you purpose in your life, perspective on your troubles, and anticipation for what God has planned for you in eternity.

*How does your hope of heaven change
your perspective for living here on earth?*

He Is in Control

Do not be afraid of the terrors of the night,
nor the arrow that flies in the day.
Do not dread the disease that stalks in
darkness, nor the disaster that strikes at
midday. ... If you make the LORD your refuge,
if you make the Most High your shelter,
no evil will conquer you.

PSALM 91:5-6, 9-10

Life can be downright frightening. War, terrorism, natural disasters, disease, random accidents, and gloomy predictions for the future can terrify and overwhelm us. Yet you can't live your life or lead others in a constant state of panic.

It's comforting to remember that God is still in control of the world and the universe, and he protects you more than you are probably aware of. Even more important than protecting your body, God promises to protect your soul.

Are you able to entrust your future—
here on earth and ultimately in heaven—
to God's care?

Courage to Move Ahead

Be strong and courageous!
Do not be afraid or discouraged.
For the LORD your God is with you wherever you go.

JOSHUA 1:9

The LORD will go ahead of you; yes, the God
of Israel will protect you from behind.

ISAIAH 52:12

As a leader, you may sometimes feel as if you are alone or that you are sailing into uncharted waters. The greatest encouragement is knowing that God is with you each step of the way. Even more than that, God has gone before you to prepare the hearts and minds of those you will interact with, and he is also behind you, protecting your back. He is with you, behind you, and ahead of you. Wherever you go, you are encircled by the almighty God!

Do you need more courage to move ahead in
a difficult situation you are facing? With God's
presence encircling you, what is stopping you?

A Servant Heart

*You must have the same attitude
that Christ Jesus had. Though he was God,
he did not think of equality with God
as something to cling to. Instead,
he gave up his divine privileges. ...
When he appeared in human form,
he humbled himself in obedience to God
and died a criminal's death on a cross.*

PHILIPPIANS 2:5-8

Many believe wealth and success mean being able to afford the luxury of having servants. Jesus turns this thinking on its head by teaching that the highest goal in life is to be a servant, because it is centered on others rather than yourself and is the essence of effective Christian leadership.

When you develop an attitude of service, Jesus will turn your humble actions into something profound and purposeful. You aren't just doing work anymore; you are impacting people's lives.

*In what ways can you serve
the people you lead today?*

No Wasted Sorrow

In my distress I prayed to the LORD,
and the LORD answered me and set me free.

We know that God causes everything
to work together for the good of those
who love God and are called according
to his purpose for them.

ROMANS 8:28

The universal human response to tragedy or calamity is grief. The Bible teaches that Christians—who live in relationship with God through Jesus Christ—also grieve during times of loss, but we grieve with hope.

We grieve because we experience the real pain of loss, but we grieve with hope because we know that God can and will turn our tragedy into something good for his glory. God promises not to waste our sorrows.

Are you able to grieve with hope?
When you do, you will help others find hope too.

With You in Troubles

When you go through deep waters,
I will be with you.
When you go through rivers of difficulty,
you will not drown. When you walk through
the fire of oppression, you will not be burned up;
the flames will not consume you.

ISAIAH 43:2

When you are faced with great adversity, you may ask, "Where is God now, when I need him most?" The answer is always the same—God is right beside you. The heavenly Father is there, and he has the power to help you cope.

God doesn't promise to save you from trouble in this life. Instead, God promises to be with you in your troubles, give you endurance to cope, strength to overcome your problems, and understanding to see how you are maturing as you learn to deal with adversity.

The next time troubles overwhelm you,
focus on how God will help you through
them instead of how to escape them.

Using What You Have

*God blesses those who are poor
and realize their need for him,
for the Kingdom of Heaven is theirs.*

MATTHEW 5:3

Contentment comes when you are willing to give up everything for God. It doesn't mean that you have to give it all up but that you are willing to.

Only then are you truly free to relax in the peace and security God offers.

Contentment is not about how much you have but about what you do for God with what you do have.

* * *

*Is there anything you are not
willing to give up for God?*

A Mentoring Relationship

You have heard me teach things that have been confirmed by many reliable witnesses. Now teach these truths to other trustworthy people who will be able to pass them on to others. ... The Lord will help you understand all these things.

2 TIMOTHY 2:2, 7

A mentoring relationship is specifically intended for teaching and learning. Good mentors commit to building a relationship with someone who is younger or has less life experience. Through this relationship, the mentor shares wisdom, life experience, and support in hopes of helping the mentee learn and grow.

Similarly, Christ sent us the Holy Spirit as our ultimate spiritual mentor. It is through the Holy Spirit that Christ helps us build a relationship with God and guides us into wisdom, maturity, and understanding.

Are you mentoring someone and passing along the wisdom God has given you?

Demonstrating Godly Character

Suppose a certain man is righteous and does what is just and right. He stays away from injustice, is honest and fair when judging others, and faithfully obeys my decrees and regulations. Anyone who does these things is just and will surely live, says the Sovereign LORD.

EZEKIEL 18:5-9

People often argue that a leader's personal life doesn't really matter as long as he or she performs well on the job.

The Father, however, does not make a distinction between your public and private life. Justice, mercy, integrity, righteousness, honesty, fairness, and faithfulness are essential traits of a godly character.

They demonstrate that you understand what is truly important in life—loving, honoring, and respecting God and others.

———— • ————

Do you demonstrate a godly character in all aspects of your life?

Get Organized

*When you meet together, one will sing,
another will teach, another will tell some
special revelation God has given,
one will speak in tongues,
and another will interpret what is said.
But everything that is done must strengthen
all of you. ... For God is not a God of disorder
but of peace, as in all the meetings
of God's holy people.*

1 CORINTHIANS 14:26, 33

Leaders know that accomplishment through community requires organization in order to prevent chaos and mishaps. Leaders help everyone understand their individual roles within the group.

Taking time to organize and train people shows that you value the people involved and helps them utilize their gifts and abilities to the fullest. Getting organized allows God's people to complete the tasks he has given them to do.

*How could you implement better organization
in order to accomplish more for God?*

Used for Good Purposes

*My dear brothers and sisters ... you died to
the power of the law when you died with Christ.
And now you are united with the one who was
raised from the dead. As a result, we can
produce a harvest of good deeds for God.*

ROMANS 7:4

God wastes nothing but instead uses everything
to further his good purposes. He will use you in
whatever situation your find yourself, and he will use
your circumstances to prepare you for future service.
If you feel like your current role isn't significant,
remember that God is preparing you for service in
the future.

Make the most of where God has put you right
now because he wants to use you both now and
later. Serving God right where you are will prepare
you for where God eventually wants to move you.

*What can you do right now
to be most effective for God?*

Live by His Standards

The LORD detests the use of dishonest scales,
but he delights in accurate weights.

PROVERBS 11:1

If you want God's blessing, you must live by his standards of fairness and justice. Cheating is the opposite of honesty. The motive behind it is always to deceive someone else.

How can a cheater be trusted? The cheater always becomes the loser, gaining something insignificant at the cost of godly character, integrity, and peace of mind.

———— • ————

In what way, no matter how small,
might you be cheating someone else or
even God? Is it ultimately worth it?

A Wellspring of Wisdom

*Anyone who listens to my teaching and
follows it is wise, like a person who builds
a house on solid rock.*

MATTHEW 7:24

How can you make wise decisions at a moment's notice? The key is to be prepared by developing wisdom over time. One way you do that is by keeping yourself pure—filling your mind with God's words instead of the world's advice.

You can't anticipate everything that might happen today, but when you are prepared spiritually—when you have developed godly wisdom—you will know the right thing to do so God can use you to accomplish good. You will be ready to act swiftly and decisively because you have a wellspring of wisdom to draw upon.

*Are you preparing today so you
can act with wisdom tomorrow?*

When Panic Strikes

*When the earth quakes and its people
live in turmoil, I am the one who keeps
its foundations firm.*

PSALM 75:3

*God is our refuge and strength,
always ready to help in times of trouble.
So we will not fear when earthquakes come
and the mountains crumble into the sea.*

PSALM 46:1-2

Panic is physically and emotionally paralyzing—
worry and fear meet in instant crisis. You've had no
time to prepare for it, and you're too frozen with fear
to deal with it.

If you haven't experienced panic before or if you
haven't prepared for it, you won't be able to deal well
with it when it hits. The closer you are to God, the
better able you are to tap into his courage and peace
when panic strikes. Then you will have a clear head
and you can act with purpose.

How do you respond when panic strikes?

Peace Out of Chaos

Give all your worries and cares to God,
for he cares about you.

1 PETER 5:7

Taste and see that the LORD is good.
Oh, the joys of those who take refuge in him!

PSALM 34:8

Have you ever been late for an appointment because you were stuck in traffic? Has it ever rained every day of your long-awaited vacation? Have you lost a good friend? Sooner or later, we all face situations beyond our control.

The Bible teaches that when you find yourself in unpredictable, uncontrollable, and frustrating circumstances, there is one thing you can control—your reaction to the situation. You can trust God to work in your life to bring order, hope, and peace out of chaos.

What are you experiencing right now
that is beyond your control?
How can you give it over to God?

Confronted by Truth

Don't lie to each other, for you have stripped off your old sinful nature and all its wicked deeds. Put on your new nature, and be renewed as you learn to know your Creator and become like him.

COLOSSIANS 3:9-10

There are times when people need to hear the hard truth rather than a pep talk. Often people seek advice from those who will confirm their own sinful desires and encourage them in destructive or unhealthy behaviors.

As a leader, your words of truth might be just what someone needs to hear in order to turn from sin. So don't be afraid to speak the truth. When you speak honestly out of the new nature you have in Christ, you will be able to speak truth to the other person's heart.

Do you know someone who needs to be confronted—gently but firmly— with God's truth?

Constructive Criticism

If you listen to constructive criticism,
you will be at home among the wise.
If you reject discipline, you only harm yourself;
but if you listen to correction,
you grow in understanding.

PROVERBS 15:31-32

Leaders are more visible and therefore more vulnerable to criticism. Much of it is unfounded, but the Bible promises that gaining wisdom depends on accepting criticism. If it comes from a credible person, humble yourself and consider the input.

Just as a coach helps an athlete, constructive criticism can help you on your pathway to becoming everything God wants you to be.

How do you typically respond to criticism?
Would the people you lead agree?
Do you have the courage and humility
to ask them?

Open Your Heart

Always think carefully before pronouncing judgment. Remember that you do not judge to please people but to please the LORD. He will be with you when you render the verdict in each case. Fear the LORD and judge with integrity, for the LORD our God does not tolerate perverted justice, partiality, or the taking of bribes.

2 CHRONICLES 19:6-7

When you live as though this world is all there is, you deceive yourself into thinking you can ignore God and still receive his blessings. Sooner or later, this deception will catch up with you. Don't let the pursuit of pleasure and materialism blind you to the realities of God's wisdom, guidance, holiness, and justice. When you allow your heart to be open to God's Word, his truth breaks through and helps you see your life from his perspective.

Make a list of the five qualities you focus on cultivating as a leader. Is justice one of them?

Do You Have a Cold Heart?

*What sorrow awaits you shepherds who
feed yourselves instead of your flocks.
Shouldn't shepherds feed their sheep? …
You have not taken care of the weak.
You have not tended the sick
or bound up the injured. You have
not gone looking for those who
have wandered away and are lost.*

EZEKIEL 34:2-4

A lack of compassion hurts the people God has placed in your life. It causes your heart to grow cold. A cold heart is a dead heart.

If you find yourself thinking mostly about your own needs and desires, your heart is losing the compassion that makes you effective for God and keeps you spiritually and emotionally healthy.

*What can you do to make sure you are
becoming a more compassionate leader?*

A Humble Heart

Then Jesus said to his disciples,
"If any of you wants to be my follower,
you must turn from your selfish ways,
take up your cross, and follow me."

MATTHEW 16:24

There's a difference between wanting to be a part of God's great work and wanting personal greatness through God's work. If you're not sure which is true for you, examine your motives. If the primary benefactor of your achievements is yourself, then perhaps you are trying to find greatness in the wrong way.

If the primary benefactor of your work is others, then you have discovered the essence of true greatness: humility. Only through humility can you rise above petty selfishness to make a difference in the lives of others and understand how valuable you are to God. Pride tries to elevate you above others, but when you humble yourself, God elevates you.

Do you spend more time thinking about
what you will get or what you will give?

Always Available

If I go up to heaven, you are there;
if I go down to the grave, you are there.
If I ride the wings of the morning,
if I dwell by the farthest oceans,
even there your hand will guide me,
and your strength will support me.

PSALM 139:8-10

God's presence is available to help you at any moment and in any place. He is always with you, always listening to you, always pursuing you with his love. Remember this promise of God when the pressure's on and you feel like you're on your own.

How can you remind yourself that
God is available to help you anytime?

OCTOBER

Where Do You Belong?

No one can serve two masters.
For you will hate one and love the other;
you will be devoted to one and despise the other.

MATTHEW 6:24

You cannot belong to both God and the world. When you belong to the world, you will pursue worldly pleasures, which are self-indulgent. When you belong to God, you will want to say and do things that conflict with what the culture values.

As a leader, it is important to stay focused and not let your energies become divided between two opposing sides. Decide today who you belong to.

Would the people who know you say
you belong to the world or to God?

A Painless Eternal Future

We believers also groan, even though we have the Holy Spirit within us as a foretaste of future glory, for we long for our bodies to be released from sin and suffering.

ROMANS 8:23

Trusting God does not produce a storybook life in which every problem is quickly resolved. Sometimes people get sick and don't get better; relationships break down and can't be reconciled; jobs are lost and not regained. When Jesus returns, there will be no more discomfort, disappointment, disease, pain, or death, and you will live in God's joy forever.

Because this happy ending is certain, you can endure the pain of unanswered questions and unending crises in this life. This hope offers you a dose of strength to help you through every day until eternity.

Do you have the strength to look beyond your present pain to your painless eternal future?

Well-Placed Confidence

Don't be afraid, for I am with you. Don't be discouraged, for I am your God. I will strengthen you and help you. I will hold you up with my victorious right hand.

ISAIAH 41:10

Over the course of your lifetime, you and those you lead will face many frightening situations. True courage comes from understanding that God is stronger than your biggest problem or your worst enemy, and he wants you to use his power to help you.

Courage is not misplaced confidence in your own strength; it is well-placed confidence in God's strength. Fear comes from feeling alone against a great threat, but courage comes from knowing that God is beside you, helping you fight. When you have courage, you can focus more on God's presence and less on the problem.

What major problem do you need the courage to face today? Can you sense God's presence beside you?

His Love Is Never Lost

*I am convinced that nothing can ever separate
us from God's love. Neither death nor life,
neither angels nor demons, neither our fears
for today nor our worries about tomorrow—not
even the powers of hell can separate us from
God's love. No power in the sky above or in the
earth below—indeed, nothing in all creation will
ever be able to separate us from the love of God
that is revealed in Christ Jesus our Lord.*

ROMANS 8:38-39

There is nothing more powerful than God's love
for you. He promises that you will never lose his love,
his presence, or his promise of salvation—the three
greatest gifts he has given you to see you through
life's difficulties and give you hope.

*No matter what loss you are grieving,
take comfort that you will never lose God's love.*

Restrain Anger

"Listen, you rebels!" [Moses] shouted.
"Must we bring you water from this rock?"
Then Moses raised his hand and struck
the rock twice with the staff,
and water gushed out. ...
But the LORD said to Moses and Aaron,
"Because you did not trust me enough
to demonstrate my holiness to the people
of Israel, you will not lead
them into the land I am giving them!"

NUMBERS 20:10-12

The pressures of leadership often try one's patience to the limit. The persistent complaints and accusations of the Israelites pushed Moses beyond his limit. He reacted in anger and deliberately disobeyed God, which cost him the fulfillment of his mission to lead God's people into the Promised Land. Failure to restrain your anger may mean failure to realize your God-given dreams.

What steps can you take to
restrain inappropriate anger?

A Fair Evaluation

*Don't let them waste their time in endless
discussion of myths and spiritual pedigrees.
These things only lead to meaningless speculations,
which don't help people live a life of faith in God.
The purpose of my instruction is that
all believers would be filled with love
that comes from a pure heart,
a clear conscience, and genuine faith.*

1 TIMOTHY 1:4-5

Leaders have the difficult task of evaluating people
to determine their fitness for particular tasks and responsibilities. This may seem judgmental, but it isn't.

Evaluation is about determining a person's fitness for service and discerning areas for growth and
development. You can know that you are evaluating your workers by the right standards when their
work is productive and done with integrity.

*How can you make sure you are evaluating
people fairly, not judging them?*

Serve Enthusiastically

I will be filled with joy because of you.
I will sing praises to your name,
O Most High.

Some aspects of the Christian life we view with appropriate seriousness—sin and its consequences, church discipline, fighting against evil.

But the Christian life also holds great delights—the knowledge that the God of the universe loves you, has a plan for you, and has made this wonderful world for you to live in. In fact, God wants you to serve him enthusiastically, joyfully, and with great delight. God promises to fill you with the joy he delights to see in his followers. He understands that enthusiasm lights the fire of service.

———— • ————

Are you enthusiastic about your
faith and your work? How can
you let others see your joy?

Qualified by God

*It is not that we think we are qualified
to do anything on our own.
Our qualification comes from God.*

2 CORINTHIANS 3:5

Power is intoxicating; with it comes recognition, control, and often wealth. These can feed pride, and pride leads us away from God and into sin. This is why power so often corrupts.

If you are in a position of power or authority, two things will help you use it wisely: accountability and service. When you have to explain your motives to others, you will be more careful about what you do and say. And when you serve others instead of yourself with your power, you will gain support and loyalty from the people in your care.

How are you using your power as a leader?

A Clear Conscience

Cling to your faith in Christ, and keep your
conscience clear. For some people have
deliberately violated their consciences;
as a result, their faith has been shipwrecked.

1 TIMOTHY 1:19

God says that if you ignore your conscience, your faith will be shipwrecked. When you sin, you are deliberately going against your conscience. You know that what you are doing is wrong because your conscience tells you it is, but you do it anyway because sin is often so appealing.

If you continually do what your conscience tells you not to do, eventually you will no longer hear it warning you of danger. Without a strong conscience, you become desensitized to sin and your heart becomes hardened. The key to a healthy conscience is faith in Jesus Christ.

Have you been listening to your conscience
or ignoring it? Your answer may be
an indication of the condition of your faith.

A Process of Growth

The LORD is my light and my salvation—
so why should I be afraid?
The LORD is my fortress, protecting me
from danger, so why should I tremble?

PSALM 27:1

Growth and success occur through taking risks. This does not excuse taking foolish chances, but it does mean that you can call upon God when stepping out in faith puts you in a difficult place.

Living by faith is a process of growth. It is a life of adventure, which also brings risk. God doesn't promise material success with every risk you take, but he does guarantee that if you live the adventure of a faithful life with him at your side, you can never be snatched away by Satan. Your eternal destiny is safe.

———— • ————

What are you willing to risk to serve God?

Crises Don't Last

Humble yourselves under the mighty power of God, and at the right time he will lift you up in honor. Give all your worries and cares to God, for he cares about you. Stay alert! Watch out for your great enemy, the devil. He prowls around like a roaring lion, looking for someone to devour. Stand firm against him, and be strong in your faith. ... After you have suffered a little while, [God] will restore, support, and strengthen you, and he will place you on a firm foundation.

1 PETER 5:6-10

Wise leaders avoid many crises by leading with humility, dependence on God, and awareness of our spiritual enemy.

Wise leaders also understand that suffering will not last forever and that God will bring restoration out of crisis. This offers hope and motivation to those you lead.

How do you avoid crises through your leadership practices?

Reaching Out

Those who live to please the Spirit will harvest everlasting life from the Spirit. So let's not get tired of doing what is good. At just the right time we will reap a harvest of blessing if we don't give up. Therefore, whenever we have the opportunity, we should do good to everyone— especially to those in the family of faith.

GALATIANS 6:8-10

It's easy to like people who are likable, but you model God's love more when you show love to those who are unlovable. There are no perfect people. But you can take joy in loving those imperfect people God has placed in your sphere of influence.

God can bring the most unlikely individuals together to have a great impact. When you reach out to others in love, your own heart will be changed.

Do the people you lead need to experience more of God's love through you?

Using Your Authority Right

*It is not that we think we are qualified
to do anything on our own.
Our qualification comes from God.*

2 CORINTHIANS 3:5

Authority will either corrupt you so you want to enrich only yourself, or empower you so you want to enrich others. If you are in a position of authority, be sure to incorporate accountability and service into your leadership style.

Then you will be careful about what you do and say and serve others instead of yourself. Not only will you gain support and loyalty from the people you lead, you will empower them to do good for others.

How are you using your authority?

Living by God's Rules

What sorrow for those who are wise in their own eyes and think themselves so clever.

ISAIAH 5:21

We all have areas in our lives where we want to be in charge and make our own rules. But just as there is room for only one driver in a car, so there is room for only one God in your heart.

Try to discover those areas in your life where you are still making the rules instead of living by God's rules. These are the areas where you need to give up control to him. When you do, you will save yourself much grief by avoiding a fight with God—a battle the Bible promises you cannot and should not win.

In what areas of life are you having trouble giving up control to God?

A Daily Challenge

I have hidden your word in my heart,
that I might not sin against you.

PSALM 119:11

Each day presents you with new choices. A choice that you can always make is to honor God and obey his Word. This one decision will always point you toward God's ways and put you squarely in the center of his will.

It will be easier for you to make this choice when you are reading God's Word, seeking his guidance through prayer and the advice of godly counselors, and avoiding choices that benefit you at the expense of others. Making the choice is not complicated, but it is a daily challenge.

What choices are your top priorities today?

Bring Your Concerns to Him

I love the LORD because he hears my voice and my prayer for mercy.

PSALM 116:1

Give all your worries and cares to God, for he cares about you.

1 PETER 5:7

God cares for you. He does not ignore a single prayer, no matter how simple it may be. When you bring your burdens to God in prayer, you will often experience real freedom from worry and anxiety in your heart and soul because you are confident that God cares and listens to you.

The promise of God's love and concern refreshes you and renews your hope.

How often do you bring your concerns to God in prayer?

Maximizing Your Abilities

*It is not that we think we are qualified
to do anything on our own.
Our qualification comes from God.*

2 CORINTHIANS 3:5

When you use your God-given abilities, you will feel more joy and fulfillment in life. So rejoice in your abilities, but let that rejoicing be poured out as a thank offering to the God who gave them to you.

Without God, your abilities would be like dreams without power, cups without water, or engines without fuel.

*Can you list your God-given abilities?
How can you maximize them today?*

You Can Count on Me

*Oh, the joys of those who do not follow the advice
of the wicked, or stand around with sinners,
or join in with mockers. But they delight
in the law of the LORD, meditating on it day
and night. They are like trees planted along
the riverbank, bearing fruit each season.
Their leaves never wither,
and they prosper in all they do.*

PSALM 1:1-3

Faithfulness says, "You can count on me—I will never let you down." There is nothing like the faithfulness of another to build your sense of security in your relationship with that person. And there is nothing like the faithfulness of God to build your confidence in your eternal security.

Faithfulness determines the quality of your character, which affects the quality of your life and brings vitality and productivity to your work.

*How is your faithfulness positively
affecting the quality of your life?*

Don't Compromise Faith

*Be very careful never to make a treaty
with the people who live in the land where
you are going. If you do, you will follow
their evil ways and be trapped.*

EXODUS 34:12

This seems like a strange promise, but it points out the danger of falling into a lifestyle of sin. This is particularly dangerous for leaders, who live and work with greater temptation to compromise.

God knows that certain behaviors not only harm you physically but also put your soul in mortal danger. That is why God warns you not to compromise with the evil that surrounds you. If you do, you will soon be living comfortably with sin rather than struggling to be true to God and his Word.

---

*How can you live and lead in today's culture
without compromising your convictions?*

Replace Judgment with Mercy

You will be treated as you treat others. The standard you use in judging is the standard by which you will be judged.

MATTHEW 7:2

You will be judged by the same standard you use, so it's better to be merciful and forgiving than harsh and critical. Before you jump to conclusions about someone, it helps to remember how you've been hurt when others have wrongfully judged you. This will broaden your perspective and help you avoid looking at other people through a negative filter that distorts their reputation.

See others as Jesus sees them—as God's children worthy of love and kindness—and replace judgment with mercy.

———————•———————

Can you think of a time you misjudged someone? How can you avoid doing that again?

His Way Is Best

Their command is a lamp and their instruction a light; their corrective discipline is the way to life.

PROVERBS 6:23

God's way is the best way to live. And God's way is clearly spelled out in the Bible.

A life of joy, satisfaction, and purpose doesn't just happen, however. It takes a plan. And self-discipline keeps you following your plan. It is the light that helps you keep the goal of obeying God's Word right in front of you so you don't forget it.

How can you develop the self-discipline to regularly read and apply God's Word?

Creatively Made

*We are God's masterpiece. He has created us
anew in Christ Jesus, so we can do the
good things he planned for us long ago.*

God created you to do good things, and to do good things you must be creative. Creativity is built into every human being. God wants you to use the unique gifts he fashioned in you to help and serve others. He gives you the gift of creativity so that you can express yourself in potentially millions of different ways—through worship, singing, loving, helping, playing music, crafting things, thinking through problems.

You should strive to express your creativity in God-honoring ways because it is an extension of a characteristic of God. When the expression of your creativity accomplishes the work God has in mind for you, you are a masterpiece, a beautiful expression of God's image doing God's work for God's people.

*How are you using your creativity to
accomplish what God created you to do?*

God Approves

They cried out to you and were saved.
They trusted in you and were never disgraced.

PSALM 22:5

Disappointment in some form may haunt you almost every day. If you let disappointment dominate your thoughts, you will become negative, sad, and depressed. But if you see disappointment as an opportunity for improvement, then disappointment can be put into perspective.

God doesn't want you to dwell on what could have been but on what can be. He is the God of hope. That's why he sent his Son, Jesus, to take the punishment for your disappointing behavior so you could stand before him as more than good enough. You are holy in his eyes! The next time you feel disappointed, remember everything you have, use the time to grow, and be happy that you have the approval of the One who really matters.

God wants to turn your disappointments
into victories; how can you help him?

Your Heart
Follows Your Money

Wherever your treasure is,
there the desires of your heart will also be.

MATTHEW 6:21

The Bible gives us many examples of wealthy people who loved God—Abraham, David, Joseph of Arimathea, Lydia. And it doesn't condemn them for their wealth. Scripture doesn't focus on how much money you have but on what you do with it. Jesus made one thing clear: Wherever your money goes, your heart will follow after it.

It's fine for you to work hard and succeed without guilt. But make sure you work just as hard at finding ways to please God with your money. Otherwise your money might lead your heart away from God.

———— • ————

How do you spend your money?
What does that say about your heart?

What Will the Outcome Be?

Don't be misled. ... You will always harvest what you plant. Those who live only to satisfy their own sinful nature will harvest decay and death from that sinful nature. But those who live to please the Spirit will harvest everlasting life from the Spirit.

GALATIANS 6:7-8

A consequence is an outcome, aftermath, or result. Some actions produce consequences that are neither morally good nor bad. For example, if you take a shower, you will get clean. But many thoughts and actions have definite good or bad consequences. Sin will always cause bad consequences.

Faithfulness to God will always result in good consequences. Before you act, ask yourself, *What will the consequences of my actions be?*

———— • ————

Have you thought through the consequences of what you plan to do and say today?

Preparing Your Mind

I wait quietly before God, for my victory comes from him. ... Let all that I am wait quietly before God, for my hope is in him.

PSALM 62:1, 5

Meditation is setting aside time to intentionally think about God, talk to him, and listen to him. When you make time to meditate on God, you distance yourself from the distractions and noise of the world and move within range of his voice. You prepare your mind to be taught and your desires to be molded into what God desires.

As a result, God promises to change you, and your thoughts and actions will fall in line with his will. Meditation is more than just the study of God. It is intimate communion with him, which ultimately leads to godly living.

How can you make it a daily habit to meditate on God?

Recognize His Leading

Trust in the LORD with all your heart;
do not depend on your own understanding.
Seek his will in all you do, and he will show
you which path to take.

PROVERBS 3:5-6

If you walk within God's will today and every day, you can be sure that you will be walking in his will twenty years from now. God's will for you is to obey him, serve others, read his Word, and do what is right.

When you are faithful over time, there comes a point when it feels as if God is letting you choose which way to go. It is then that you have grown close enough to God to recognize his leading in your life.

What can you do to follow
God's will more closely today?

Victory Over Evil

*This I declare about the LORD: He alone is
my refuge, my place of safety; he is my God,
and I trust him. ... His faithful promises are your
armor and protection. Do not be afraid of
the terrors of the night, nor the arrow that
flies in the day. ... For he will order his angels
to protect you wherever you go.*

PSALM 91:2-5, 11

This passage of Scripture has been a constant source of courage and encouragement for God's people throughout the centuries. It reminds you that although the threats in this world seem endless, the promise of the heavenly Father's eternal protection is infinitely greater.

Sooner or later your earthly body will die, but God promises that he will never let evil conquer or enslave his followers for eternity.

*How does knowing that God has victory
over evil help you to live courageously now?*

Jesus Is on Your Side

If the world hates you, remember that it hated me first. The world would love you as one of its own if you belonged to it, but you are no longer part of the world. I chose you to come out of the world, so it hates you.

JOHN 15:18-19

If God is for us, who can ever be against us?

ROMANS 8:31

Evil can't stand the sight of Jesus, can't bear even to hear his name. If you are living in a way that others can clearly see Jesus in you, there is good news and bad news. The bad news is that you will face opposition and even persecution for your faith.

Satan opposes Jesus, so if you are for Jesus, you have an enemy in Satan. The good news is that with Jesus on your side, you cannot lose the battle for your soul. Even if the whole world is against you, God is for you. He promises to give you spiritual victories in this life and ultimate victory for eternity.

Are you experiencing any spiritual opposition?

The Battle for Your Soul

*Put on all of God's armor so that you will
be able to stand firm against all strategies
of the devil. For we are not fighting against
flesh-and-blood enemies, but against evil rulers
and authorities of the unseen world, against
mighty powers in this dark world, and
against evil spirits in the heavenly places.*

EPHESIANS 6:10-12

Leaders are especially vulnerable to spiritual attacks because they influence many others. If Satan can conquer your heart and turn you against God, he might get many others to turn away as well.

So the battle is over your very soul, and you must fight with all your strength and with every weapon God provides for you. You cannot fight Satan alone. You must use the armor God has given you. The devil specializes in putting obstacles in your path, but the Father specializes in helping you overcome them.

*What weapons are you using to
defend yourself from spiritual attacks?*

Realize His Power

O LORD, I have so many enemies; so many
are against me. ... But you, O LORD,
are a shield around me; you are my glory,
the one who holds my head high. ...
Victory comes from you, O LORD.

PSALM 3:1, 3, 8

The powers of evil can seem overwhelming at times. You may wonder how you can keep going. But God says not to be afraid because he will act like a shield around you.

When you are afraid, the courage you need comes only from realizing how powerful God is. Then the odds won't seem so impossible. No enemy can stand before him. God is more powerful than any force against you.

Are you feeling overwhelmed?
How can you learn to trust God for victory?

NOVEMBER

Step Out in Faith

My ambition has always been to preach the Good News where the name of Christ has never been heard. ... I have been following the plan spoken of in the Scriptures, where it says, "Those who have never been told about him will see, and those who have never heard of him will understand."

ROMANS 15:20-21

Paul claimed God's promise of salvation for people all over the world. His trust in this promise drove him to new challenges, which lead to greater growth in his relationship with God. God has called you to accomplish something for him.

Find out what it is, and accept the challenge of stepping out in faith to do it. Challenges lead you to follow God into uncharted waters so that you can accomplish something unique and wonderful for him.

Have you discovered what God is challenging you to accomplish?

A Holy Fear

How joyful are those who fear the LORD—
all who follow his ways!

PSALM 128:1

Does it seem ironic that those who "fear" the Lord actually experience more joy? Fearing God, however, is not the same as being afraid of him. If you are afraid of God, you will stay away from him. Fearing God means being awed by his power, mercy, and goodness. This draws you closer to him, within the circle of blessings he gives to all who love him.

Fear of God is like the respect you have for a beloved teacher, coach, parent, or mentor. Your respect motivates you both to do your best and to avoid doing something that would offend or hurt that person. You fear God because of his awesome power, and you love God for the way he blesses you.

How can you increase your fear of God
and experience more joy as a result?

Keep on Track

Unless the LORD builds a house,
the work of the builders is wasted.
Unless the LORD protects a city,
guarding it with sentries will do no good.
It is useless for you to work so hard
from early morning until late at night,
anxiously working for food to eat;
for God gives rest to his loved ones.

PSALM 127:1-2

As a leader, it's easy to get so absorbed with keeping others on track that you neglect to keep yourself on track. Suddenly you may realize that you are further from God than you should be.

Excluding or neglecting God will cause even your best efforts to be ultimately futile because they will have no eternal results.

Are you making the effort to keep
God at the center of your work?

An Authentic Lifestyle

You yourself must be an example to them
by doing good works of every kind.
Let everything you do reflect the integrity
and seriousness of your teaching. ...
Then those who oppose us will be ashamed
and have nothing bad to say about us.

TITUS 2:7-8

An authentic Christian lifestyle is a witness to the community at large.

What people say about the way you live will probably have the greatest impact on what they think about your leadership, your church, and even other Christians.

Your actions will either attract other people to your faith in God or turn them away.

What do you think your faith looks
like to people in your community?

The Best Example

*You are the light of the world—like a city
on a hilltop that cannot be hidden.
No one lights a lamp and then puts it
under a basket. Instead, a lamp is placed
on a stand, where it gives light to everyone
in the house. In the same way,
let your good deeds shine out for all to see,
so that everyone will praise your heavenly Father.*

MATTHEW 5:14-16

Whether you like it or not, people are always watching you. This means that you are setting an example, either good or bad, for others. You can set a good example by living out the same attitudes and actions Jesus taught and lived.

If you use Jesus Christ as your example, you won't have to worry that you are setting a bad example for others. You can be confident that they can draw closer to Jesus because of your influence.

*What kind of example have you
been demonstrating to others lately?*

Set Free to Find Meaning

*Anyone who accepts his testimony
can affirm that God is true.*

JOHN 3:33

The Bible makes it clear that absolutes do exist and that absolute truth begins with God. God's Word reveals the truths that make the world work, that make relationships work, and that determine our future. By studying these truths and living by them, we discover the way life should work.

God's truth sets us free from a meaningless and chaotic life to a certain and eternal future where life will always make sense and will always be fair and full of joy.

That is the kind of truth others will want to follow.

*How can you use what you
know is true to lead others?*

Showing Greater Care

*I will give you shepherds after my
own heart, who will guide you
with knowledge and understanding.*

JEREMIAH 3:15

As a leader, you must follow Christ's example in caring for those you lead. Good leaders keep the whole person in mind, not just productivity. They recognize and affirm the different roles and abilities of different people.

Sometimes you have to compromise and accommodate the reality of human struggles and trials. But God promises to give you a heart that guides with wisdom and expresses understanding so you can show deep care for those you lead.

*Do you need to show your people
greater care and understanding?*

Admitting Your Dependence

Humble yourselves before the Lord,
and he will lift you up in honor.

JAMES 4:10

The world says you have dignity when you are worthy of the respect and praise of others. Many people seek leadership in order to gain the power or wealth that brings them this respect. Ironically, true dignity comes not when you're honored by others but when you choose to honor God and others.

Humbly admitting your dependence on him will bring you honor and dignity in ways that really matter. Some people won't recognize this kind of dignity, but God does, and he promises to bless you for it.

What is your definition of dignity?

Finding Harmony

*Live in harmony with each other.
Let there be no divisions in the
church. Rather, be of one mind,
united in thought and purpose.*

1 CORINTHIANS 1:10

*Above all, clothe yourselves with love, which
binds us all together in perfect harmony.*

COLOSSIANS 3:14

Love brings harmony—not necessarily agreement, but harmony. Do you approach potential conflict with humility, allowing for the possibility that someone else's way may be better?

Do you really listen instead of trying to assert your opinion? Is your purpose to obey and serve the Lord rather than to do what you want to? If you can do these things, you will be putting love first, and you will find harmony with others.

*Do you need to change the
way you approach conflict?*

A Listening Ear

*So we must listen very carefully to the truth
we have heard, or we may drift away from it.*

HEBREWS 2:1

God wants to protect you from sin and trouble. That is best accomplished when you listen to his voice and obey his commands. When you refuse to listen to him, you lose touch with the One who gives you the strength to withstand the onslaught of sin.

You will become too weak to fight the temptations of sin, and you will give in and do things that could hurt you and those you love. Stay close enough to God that you will always be able to listen to him.

Would God call you a good listener?

Prayer for the Nation

*I urge you, first of all, to pray for all people.
Ask God to help them; intercede on their behalf,
and give thanks for them. Pray this way for
kings and all who are in authority so that
we can live peaceful and quiet lives marked
by godliness and dignity.*

1 TIMOTHY 2:1-2

It's important for Christians to pray for their nation because the Bible says it leads to peace. Pray for the nation to be protected by God's mighty hand. Pray for its leaders to be humble and wise, to discern right from wrong, and to champion the cause of the needy and helpless.

A nation that allows or endorses immorality is subject to judgment and will eventually collapse from the inside out. A nation that collectively worships the one true God will stand firm and live in peace.

*How can you pray for your country
and your company today?*

A Secure Foundation

Those who fear the LORD are secure;
he will be a refuge for their children.

PROVERBS 14:26

God is our refuge and strength,
always ready to help in times of trouble.

PSALM 46:1

When you strengthen your faith day by day with the truths of God's Word, you build a solid foundation that will not easily crack under pressure.

When life's battles come your way, the attacks may be strong enough to knock down some of your walls, but your foundation will remain steady and secure because God's truths are eternal. You will always have a secure foundation when you trust and fear God.

How secure do you feel?

Effective Delegation

Go and make disciples of all the nations,
baptizing them in the name of the Father
and the Son and the Holy Spirit.
Teach these new disciples to obey all the
commands I have given you.
And be sure of this: I am with you always,
even to the end of the age.

MATTHEW 28:19-20

When you stretch yourself too thin, you put yourself and others at risk. You wear yourself out, make others wait, prevent other people from having the opportunity to use their gifts, and keep others from growing spiritually through serving others. In the process, people become dissatisfied and distracted, and God's work doesn't get done.

Effective delegation benefits those to whom you assign a task because it stretches them, causes them to rely on God, helps them feel useful, and inspires them to catch the vision of their leaders.

What tasks can you delegate to benefit your
own leadership as well as those you lead?

Tap into God's Power

*Only in returning to me and resting in me
will you be saved. In quietness and
confidence is your strength.*

ISAIAH 30:15

*It is not by force nor by strength, but by my Spirit,
says the LORD of Heaven's Armies.*

ZECHARIAH 4:6

Burnout is draining and paralyzing. To avoid it, you need to take care of your body and mind by eating right, exercising, and getting plenty of rest. One of the best ways to reduce burnout is taking time out to be close to God.

When you draw close to him, you can tap into his power, strength, peace, protection, and love. This will help you stay strong and persevere through times of burnout.

---

*What can you do to draw closer
to God and avoid burnout?*

Admitting Your Need for God

Humble yourselves under the mighty power of God, and at the right time he will lift you up in honor.

1 PETER 5:6

Humility is essential for recognizing sin in your life. Pride gives the devil the key to your heart, but humility gives God your whole heart. In place of pride, you need the humility that comes from true sorrow over sin.

Humility allows you to openly admit that you need God and ask for his forgiveness—something that no proud person could do. When you give your whole heart to God, you open yourself up to being used by him at just the right time and place.

———•·———

Do you recognize sin in your life? If not, you are likely having a hard time being humble.

He Will Help You Through

The LORD is my strength and shield.
I trust him with all my heart.
He helps me, and my heart is filled with joy.

PSALM 28:7

When you ask God for help and trust that he will help, you open the lifeline to the God who loves to do the impossible for you.

If you focus only on trying to get yourself out of trouble, you will never see the amazing things the Father had planned for you. He promises to help you through your troubles and make you stronger because of them.

How can you trust God to help you more?

Valued in His Eyes

*Just as we are now like the earthly man [Adam],
we will someday be like the heavenly man [Christ].*

1 CORINTHIANS 15:49

We have all asked ourselves, "How do I measure up?" Satan tries to convince you to compare yourself to other people, to base your worth on how you compare with others in appearance, possessions, accomplishments, or social status. A better method of determining your worth is comparing yourself to God's standards.

Against his holiness, we all fall short. But when you reach out to him, nothing can compare with his grace. He makes you holy, even though you don't deserve it. In God's eyes, every person is valued and loved. Just enjoy his grace, which has no comparison!

*What kind of unhealthy comparisons
have you been making lately?*

Fulfilling Your God-Given Tasks

*I brought glory to you here on earth by
completing the work you gave me to do.
Now, Father, bring me into the glory
we shared before the world began.*

JOHN 17:4-5

*For everything there is a season,
a time for every activity under heaven.*

ECCLESIASTES 3:1

It's a mistake to allow your life to get out of balance by overemphasizing one of your responsibilities at the cost of others. God assures you there is time for everything he calls you to do. Jesus, despite his power and the needs of those around him, left much undone; yet he completed everything God had planned for him to do.

*If God were to give you a list of
responsibilities, what do you think
would be on it? Are any of those
responsibilities already on your list?*

Serving a Limitless God

Even perfection has its limits,
but your commands have no limit.

PSALM 119:96

Perfectionism can limit your ability to take action. It is not always necessary or desirable to wait for the "perfect" opportunity or the "perfect" conditions. When you obediently follow God's Word at every opportunity, you will have his unlimited love and blessing in your life.

Are you placing limits on yourself?
Learn to take advantage of what
your limitless God has to offer.

The Right Direction

About that time the disciples came to Jesus and asked, "Who is greatest in the Kingdom of Heaven?" ... He said, "I tell you the truth, unless you turn from your sins and become like little children, you will never get into the Kingdom of Heaven."

MATTHEW 18:1-4

Competition can be a foothold for pride and jealousy because it often leads you to compare yourself with others. Everyone has equal worth in God's eyes. Anytime you begin to think of yourself as more important or better than others, your competitive spirit is taking you in the wrong direction.

When humility tempers your competitive nature, you give everything you have to doing your best, not besting others. That, Jesus promises, is the mark of true greatness.

When you compete, are you fueled by pride or tempered by humility?

Extend Mercy

God blesses those who are merciful,
for they will be shown mercy.

MATTHEW 5:7

Mercy can be defined as compassion poured out on needy people. But the mercy of God, which he expects us to model, goes one step further. God's mercy is undeserved favor. Even when you don't deserve mercy, he still extends it. Your sin and rebellion against God deserve his punishment. But instead of punishment, he promises you forgiveness and eternal life if you simply accept his mercy.

Just as God has been merciful to you despite your sin, you should extend mercy toward those who have wronged you.

Have you accepted God's mercy and
extended the same kind of mercy
to those who have hurt you?

Opened Doors

*I know all the things you do,
and I have opened a door for you
that no one can close.*

REVELATION 3:8

You can trust that God knows your abilities. He places specific opportunities before you and gives you the tools you need to accept and fulfill them.

When God opens a door, it will stay open as long as he wants; no person can close it. But you must walk through the open door!

*What door of opportunity has God opened
for you recently? Have you walked through it yet?*

Allow the Spirit to Work

*The Holy Spirit produces this kind of fruit
in our lives: love, joy, peace, patience,
kindness, goodness, faithfulness,
gentleness, and self-control.
There is no law against these things!*

GALATIANS 5:22-23

How often do you jump to conclusions, making assumptions you later learn were wrong? When you overreact, do you tend to say and do things you regret, causing hurt and pain to others and ultimately to yourself?

The Bible promises that when you allow the Holy Spirit to work in you, the result is peace, patience, gentleness, and self-control among other things. When you do overreact, the Holy Spirit gives you the humility and courage to apologize and prevent hard feelings from escalating into open conflict.

*Have you overreacted to something lately?
Have you asked the Holy Spirit to
help you make things right?*

More Thankful
Each Day

*Giving thanks is a sacrifice that truly
honors me. If you keep to my path,
I will reveal to you the salvation of God.*

PSALM 50:23

When you give thanks to God, you honor and praise him for what he has done—in your life, in the lives of others, in the church, and in the world.

Similarly, you honor others when you thank them. It shows respect for who they are and what they have done. This attitude of gratitude prevents you from expecting others to serve you and allows you to enjoy whatever blessings come your way.

Are you becoming more thankful each day?

Give Thanks Always

Since everything God created is good, we should not reject any of it but receive it with thanks.

1 TIMOTHY 4:4

Cultivate thankfulness by regularly giving thanks to God, either alone or with others. Set aside time every day to meditate on the things you are thankful for.

Make a mental list of God's blessings in your life, and thank him for them. Don't wait until you feel thankful before you give thanks. Giving thanks will lead you to feel thankful.

Are you cultivating a thankful heart toward God and toward others?

Sing Praise

The master was full of praise. "Well done,
my good and faithful servant.
You have been faithful in handling
this small amount, so now I will give you many
more responsibilities. Let's celebrate together!"

MATTHEW 25:21

A key role of a leader is to bless those who work for you. Blessing can take the form of saying thank you to the people in your group or organization. Withholding praise or well-deserved remuneration cheats people out of recognition and affirmation, which are two of the ways people are motivated to continue serving with purpose and energy.

Appropriate praise and affirmation does not give people a big head, but it does enlarge their hearts and deepen their commitment to their leaders and the mission of the organization.

How can you bless the people you lead?

Sharing Resources

God loved the world so much that he gave his one and only Son, so that everyone who believes in him will not perish but have eternal life.

JOHN 3:16

Ever since we were little children, we've been taught to share. Yet for most of us, it remains as hard as ever to share either our things or ourselves. Why? Because at the very core of our sinful human nature is the desire to get, not give; to accumulate, not relinquish; to look out for ourselves, not for others.

The Bible calls you to share your resources, your faith, your love, your time, your talents, your money. It promises that those who share generously will discover the benefits of giving, which are far greater than the temporary satisfaction of receiving. God was willing to share his own Son with you so that you could have eternal life. When you realize how much God has shared with you, you will be more willing to share with others.

What do you have that you can share generously with others?

The Condition of Your Heart

*Wherever your treasure is,
there the desires of your heart will also be.*

LUKE 12:34

In the Bible, the heart is considered the center of thought and feeling. God cautions you to guard it above all else (see Proverbs 4:23) because your heart filters everything that happens to you and around you. When you neglect your heart, it becomes filthy and clogged with all kinds of foulness—bitterness, jealousy, impure thoughts.

A dirty heart can no longer distinguish the good and healthy from the harmful, so it allows hurt and heartache to enter. When you keep your heart pure and clean, it blocks sinful thoughts and desires that could destroy you. A pure heart is the best prescription for a long, happy, and healthy life, and it is essential for leadership with integrity.

When the Great Physician looks at your heart, in what condition does he find it?

A Successful Relationship

What do you benefit if you gain the whole world but lose your own soul? Is anything worth more than your soul?

MATTHEW 16:26

If you were to reach the end of your life having managed a successful business, raised a good family, won all kinds of community awards, and retired comfortably, would you say your life was a success?

God says that kind of life would be a failure if you did all those things apart from him. If you live your life apart from God now, it means you will be apart from him for eternity. And since God is good and perfect, it means you will have lived life apart from all that is good and perfect. Don't fail in the biggest way by neglecting or ignoring God. You will have success when you discover what a relationship with God means for your future.

If you were to die tomorrow and meet God face-to-face, do you think he would say your life was a success or a failure?

Keep Listening

We must listen very carefully to the truth we have heard, or we may drift away from it.

HEBREWS 2:1

"My wayward children," says the LORD, "come back to me, and I will heal your wayward hearts."

JEREMIAH 3:22

Perhaps you've suddenly realized you're farther away from God than you should be, and you're worried. Backsliding often begins with simple neglect or falling back into a sinful habit.

God promises that when you take the time and effort to really listen to him, he will show you where you've strayed and bring you back to him. If you're following him closely now, keep listening so you don't get off track from the life he wants you to live.

How can you learn to listen to God and avoid backsliding?

DECEMBER

Changed Inside-Out

*God is working in you, giving you the desire
and the power to do what pleases him.*

PHILIPPIANS 2:13

God doesn't force change on you. When you invite him into your life, you give him permission to use his power to change you. If you try to change on your own, you won't get good results, but you will get discouraged.

Instead, let the very power of God himself begin a work of transformation in you that will last a lifetime. Your life will see dramatic changes if you allow God to do his work in you.

*How can you allow God to change
you from the inside out?*

Seeing or Believing?

*Jesus told him, "You believe because you
have seen me. Blessed are those
who believe without seeing me."*

The strongest faith is based not on physical proof
but on spiritual conviction. There is a spiritual ele-
ment to this world that you cannot see but that is
very real.

Your faith becomes stronger as the Holy Spirit
sharpens your "spiritual vision" so that you can see
and experience the results of God working in your
own life and in the lives of those around you.

God promises to bless those who believe even
when their spiritual vision is weak.

Is your faith based on seeing or believing?

Devoted to the Father

You are now a slave of Christ.

1 CORINTHIANS 7:22

*Now you are free from your slavery to sin,
and you have become slaves to righteous living.*

ROMANS 6:18

*You are free, yet you are God's slaves, so don't
use your freedom as an excuse to do evil.*

1 PETER 2:16

As a believer in Jesus Christ, you are to be completely devoted to serving him—you are to be a slave, so to speak. Jesus' perfect character and his will should govern your life. Being servants or slaves of Christ is true freedom because your attachment to him detaches you from those things that would enslave you to sin and eternal death. When you serve him, you follow the only One who can set you free from sin and bring you to heaven, where you can live forever in joy and peace.

To what or whom are you most devoted?

Believing the Promises

Through Christ you have come to trust in God.
And you have placed your faith and hope
in God because he raised Christ from
the dead and gave him great glory.

1 PETER 1:21

The Lord is your source of hope because his promises are true. You'll lose hope if you stop believing that. The Resurrection, the greatest event in history, is the foundation of the hope that you have.

Jesus promised he would rise from the dead, and because he did, you can be assured that every other promise God makes to you will also come true.

Do you know which of God's promises in the
Bible apply to you? Do you believe them?
If so, how should this affect your leadership style?

There with You

*Where two or three gather together as
my followers, I am there among them.*

Joining with a community of believers not only provides an organized means of preaching and teaching
God's Word, it also provides you with a chance to regularly get together with other believers to strengthen,
encourage, and build each other up, to pray for each
other, hold each other accountable, and meet each
other's needs.

God promises to be among you whenever you
meet together with other Christians.

———— • ————

*When you gather with other believers, are
you counting on God to be there with you?*

Let Go of Hurt

Make allowance for each other's faults, and forgive anyone who offends you. Remember, the Lord forgave you, so you must forgive others.

COLOSSIANS 3:13

Forgiveness is not an option; it is a command. It is necessary for your relationship with God and your relationships with other people. Forgiveness doesn't mean that your hurt doesn't exist or doesn't matter, nor does it make everything "all right."

Forgiveness allows you to let go of your hurt and let God deal with the one who hurt you. Forgiveness frees you to move on with your life.

It's not always easy, but forgiving those who hurt you is the healthiest thing you can do for yourself.

Do you need to forgive someone who has hurt you so you can be free to move on?

Content in God

Don't love money; be satisfied with what you have. For God has said, "I will never fail you. I will never abandon you."

Contentment settles over your heart when you meditate on God's presence in your life and commit yourself to his priorities for your life.

Money and power cannot offer the peace and satisfaction that come from the contentment of a personal relationship with God. Even the richest people on earth are impoverished if they do not know God and have not experienced his blessings.

Have you been deceived into thinking you've found contentment without God?

He Can Do the Impossible

Nothing is impossible with God.

LUKE 1:37

There should be no doubt that God specializes in doing what from a human perspective is impossible. But the end of your abilities is the beginning of his.

The God who spoke all creation into being can do the impossible for you. You must believe that he can and that he wants to.

———— • ————

What impossible thing do you
need God to do for you today?

Joy for the Journey

You will show me the way of life,
granting me the joy of your presence
and the pleasures of living with you forever.

PSALM 16:11

Joy is the celebration of your walk with God. It is an inner happiness you have despite the circumstances around you because it is based on a relationship with Jesus Christ. It is peace with God.

It is realizing how privileged you are to know Jesus as Savior, to have your sins forgiven, to be friends with almighty God, and to be certain you will live forever with him in heaven. It is experiencing the dramatic change that occurs in your life when you allow the Holy Spirit to control your heart and mind. All of these things will bring you joy when you are walking with God.

How will you find joy in
your walk with God today?

Find Peace in the Right Place

You will keep in perfect peace all who trust in you, all whose thoughts are fixed on you!

ISAIAH 26:3

There are many ways to achieve peace, or the semblance of peace, but genuine peace is found only in a trusting relationship with God.

Peace is not the absence of conflict but the presence of God. Peace of mind comes as the Holy Spirit guides you into God's purposes for your life and gives you an eternal perspective.

Peace of heart comes as the Holy Spirit guides you into a productive life and comforts you in times of trouble.

Where are you looking for peace?
Are you looking in the right place?

Called to Be Different

*Don't copy the behavior and customs of this world,
but let God transform you into a new person
by changing the way you think.
Then you will learn to know God's will for you,
which is good and pleasing and perfect.*

ROMANS 12:2

It's easy to slip into the behavior and customs of the culture we live in. It takes thoughtful and purposeful resolution to live God's way.

He promises to help you do that by changing the way you think and transforming you into a person who pleases him.

It's better to live a life that pleases God than a life that pleases a culture bent on doing its own thing.

*Why does God call you to be
different, especially as a leader?*

Godly Compassion Requires Action

If you help the poor, you are lending to the LORD—and he will repay you!

PROVERBS 19:17

God promises that those who help the poor will be rewarded, both in this life and the next. God has compassion for the poor and needy, so as a follower of God, you must also have compassion for them.

Compassion that does not reach as far as your checkbook or your to-do list is not godly compassion. Godly compassion always requires action. Helping those less fortunate than you is not merely an obligation but a privilege that should bring you great joy.

———————•———————

Do you as a leader use your resources to help people who are less fortunate than you?

Dealing with Pressure

*We are pressed on every side by troubles,
but we are not crushed. We are perplexed,
but not driven to despair. We are hunted down,
but never abandoned by God. We get
knocked down, but we are not destroyed.
Through suffering, our bodies continue
to share in the death of Jesus so that the life
of Jesus may also be seen in our bodies.*

2 CORINTHIANS 4:8-10

Pressure can put tremendous stress on your health and your relationships. It can stretch you until you feel as if you will snap. But pressure can be positive if you learn to grow from it.

Just as your muscles grow when pushed beyond their limits, your wisdom and character grow when stretched by the pressures of life.

As you learn what God is teaching you in stressful times, you become better equipped to deal with pressure in the future.

———— • ————

How can you see pressure as positive?

Fully Redeemed

*Oh, what joy for those whose disobedience
is forgiven, whose sins are put out of sight.
Yes, what joy for those whose record
the LORD has cleared of sin.*

ROMANS 4:7-8

Guilt is a legitimate spiritual response to sin; regret is sorrow over the consequences of our decisions, both the sinful and the simply unfortunate. While God promises to remove the guilt of all who seek his forgiveness, he does not prevent the consequences of your sin.

It is likely that regret over those consequences that you still carry weighs you down with remorse. God sometimes uses brokenness and remorse to bring spiritual insight and growth. Ask yourself what God may be communicating to you through your regrets. If they drive you to God, your regrets can be redemptive.

*What regrets are you struggling with?
How might God redeem them?*

Biblical Leadership

*But among you it will be different.
Whoever wants to be a leader
among you must be your servant.*

MATTHEW 20:26

*For even the Son of Man came not to be served
but to serve others and to give his life
as a ransom for many.*

MARK 10:45

The biblical model of leadership is servanthood. Worldly leaders use power to get things done for themselves, but biblical leaders use power to serve those they are called to lead and care for.

Worldly leaders want to be served by others; biblical leaders want to serve others. When you model the leadership style that Jesus Christ used, you will be a biblical leader.

Whose model of leadership do you follow?

A Battle Plan for Life

The word of God is alive and powerful.
It is sharper than the sharpest two-edged sword,
cutting between soul and spirit,
between joint and marrow. It exposes
our innermost thoughts and desires.

HEBREWS 4:12

Your best offensive weapon is the Word of God. It's odd to think of the Bible as a weapon, but in it God reveals his plan of attack against the forces of evil that try to bring you down. It's your battle plan for life. If you don't read it, you won't know how to fight the battle that literally determines your destiny, both here on earth and in heaven for eternity.

Only by knowing who you are fighting, where the battle is being fought, and how to defend yourself will you be able to win. It is vital to study God's Word as much as you can. This weapon will send Satan running for cover.

How often are you using your
best offensive weapon?

A Symbol of Love

A spiritual gift is given to each of us so we can help each other. ... It is the one and only Spirit who distributes all these gifts. He alone decides which gift each person should have.

1 CORINTHIANS 12:7, 11

Why do we give gifts? Because gifts are a symbol of our love, commitment, and care for others. When we find the perfect gift for a friend or loved one, it gives us great joy to see that person delight in it.

Similarly, God handpicks special gifts for each one of us, and he takes great delight when we use those gifts responsibly and for his glory. Some of his gifts to us are spiritual gifts, unique abilities he gives to each individual.

You never use these spiritual gifts up; rather, the more you use them, the more they grow and help you make a greater contribution in your sphere of influence. They are a symbol of God's deep, personal, and attentive love and commitment to you.

What spiritual gift has God given you? How will you use it today?

Blinded by the Moment

We were crushed and overwhelmed beyond
our ability to endure, and we thought
we would never live through it. In fact,
we expected to die. But as a result,
we stopped relying on ourselves and learned
to rely only on God, who raises the dead.

2 CORINTHIANS 1:8-9

Stress can cause you to focus on what is trivial and miss what is important. As pressure forces your perspective inward, you lose the big picture. Pre-occupation with the issues of the moment blinds you to what's really important.

The key to dealing with stress is to recognize it and not be surprised when it comes. While there are many healthy and positive ways to handle stress, make sure you ask for the help of God's Spirit that he promises to provide.

How do you deal with stress?

Spiritual Endurance

*These trials will show that your faith is genuine.
It is being tested as fire tests and purifies gold—
though your faith is far more precious than
mere gold. So when your faith remains strong
through many trials, it will bring you much
praise and glory and honor on the day when
Jesus Christ is revealed to the whole world.*

1 PETER 1:7

The greatest reward for enduring through life is the prize of eternal life with God. This reward is given to all who have faith in Jesus Christ and who endure the challenges of living faithfully in the face of persecution, ridicule, or other temptations.

Just as marathon runners must build up their endurance so they can run the race and finish well, Christians must build endurance for living a life of faith and staying strong to the end. When you have built up your endurance, you will push on toward the goal of becoming more and more like Jesus.

*What are you doing to develop
your spiritual endurance?*

More Like Jesus

I have given you an example to follow.
Do as I have done to you.

JOHN 13:15

Jesus Christ is the ultimate example of how to live in a way that pleases God. To follow Jesus' example doesn't mean you need to be a traveling preacher and do miracles; instead, it means you should think his thoughts, adopt his attitudes, and live as he would live. This is an awesome goal, and it is difficult for imperfect humans to accomplish.

The key is not having the ability to be perfect but allowing Jesus to live his perfect life through you.

How can you be more like Jesus today?

Don't Waste His Love

*God showed how much he loved us by sending
his one and only Son into the world so that
we might have eternal life through him.
This is real love—not that we loved God,
but that he loved us and sent his Son
as a sacrifice to take away our sins.*

1 JOHN 4:9-10

Parents would gladly give up their own lives to save their child's life. Yet God did the unthinkable—he gave up his only child! He purposely and willingly sent Jesus to earth to live as a human, to experience the same joy and pain as you do. But then he was tortured and crucified and punished for your sins so you wouldn't have to experience that.

Could you make such a sacrifice of love? Don't let God's lavish love be wasted. Accept his gift of salvation, and embrace the Christ child with all your heart.

*What can you do to embrace the love
of Christ this Christmas season?*

Mighty to Save

For a child is born to us, a son is given to us.
The government will rest on his shoulders.
And he will be called ... Mighty God.

ISAIAH 9:6

It's hard to picture the baby Jesus as the almighty God, but he was mighty enough to create the world, live a sinless life, heal countless people, calm storms, and conquer death.

He is mighty enough to conquer your troubles, too, no matter how overwhelming your circumstances.

Do you more readily see Jesus as the baby
in the manger or as the almighty God?

The Ultimate Gift of All Time

*For God loved the world so much that he
gave his one and only Son,
so that everyone who believes in him
will not perish but have eternal life.*

JOHN 3:16

The greatest gift God gives you is his Son. Through his gift of Jesus, he also gives you the gift of eternal life. What makes these gifts so wonderful is that you don't have to work for them or earn them.

You simply believe that God has actually given you his Son and the offer of eternal life with him. Then you accept the gifts. And no one can take them away.

———— • ————

*God has given you gifts too
wonderful to keep to yourself.
Whom can you share them with?*

His Perfect Timing

*When we were utterly helpless, Christ came
at just the right time and died for us sinners.*

ROMANS 5:6

God's people had been longing for the Messiah
for centuries, yet God sent Jesus to earth at just the
right time. We may not fully understand why this was
perfect timing until we get to heaven and see God's
complete plan.

But you can be sure that God sent Jesus at the
time when the most people, both present and future,
would be reached with the Good News of salvation.

*How do you see evidence of God's
perfect timing in your life?*

Life's Greatest Gift

*The Savior—yes, the Messiah, the Lord—
has been born today in Bethlehem, the city
of David! And you will recognize him by
this sign: You will find a baby wrapped snugly
zin strips of cloth, lying in a manger.*

LUKE 2:11-12

God often accomplishes his plans in unexpected ways. He chose to have Jesus born in a stable rather than a palace; he chose tiny Bethlehem rather than Jerusalem; and he chose to proclaim the news of Jesus' birth first to shepherds rather than to kings.

Perhaps God did all this to show that life's greatest gift—salvation through Jesus Christ—is available to everyone.

Perhaps it also shows that the lowly and humble might have a better chance of receiving God's message and even leading by it.

*Is humility shaping the way
you live and lead?*

Power at Work

We now have this light shining in our hearts,
but we ourselves are like fragile clay jars
containing this great treasure.
This makes it clear that our great power
is from God, not from ourselves.

2 CORINTHIANS 4:7

Leaders are human. You get tired, frustrated, discouraged, and confused. You fail and you sin. Yet by God's grace, your humanity does not disqualify you from serving God in all that you do.

In fact, it becomes the means through which God reveals his power and mercy.

Do you see the power of God
working through your humanity?

Set Attainable Goals

Take delight in the LORD,
and he will give you your heart's desires.

PSALM 37:4

When a ship sets out on a long voyage at sea, the captain needs to plot the course. This includes choosing the route, setting the schedule, determining the places to stop, and deciding the responsibilities for each crew member.

By planning ahead and setting attainable goals, the captain ensures that the ship will stay on the right track and arrive safely at its destination. This is the role of good leaders. Setting attainable goals is necessary to give your people a destination and a course for getting there. Without goals, everyone wanders aimlessly. When you allow God to be your captain and plot your life's goals, then your goals for others will become clear as well.

What goals do you think God has for you?
How might this affect the goals you set
for the people you lead?

Share More Freely

*Wherever your treasure is,
there the desires of your heart will also be.*

MATTHEW 6:21

Who is more generous—a billionaire who gives one million dollars to the church, or a struggling single mom who gives only a hundred? If you do have a lot of money, does that mean you are not generous? Jesus says we can't know the answers to these questions without knowing the heart of the giver.

The Bible shows us that God doesn't focus on how much money you have but rather on how generous you are with it. One thing is clear: What you spend your money on reveals what you care most about. When you realize that everything you have is a gift from a generous God, it motivates you to share your money and possessions more freely.

*How might your generous giving
impact the lives of the people you lead?*

Trust God's Plans

The LORD directs our steps,
so why try to understand everything along the way?

PROVERBS 20:24

Humble yourselves before the Lord,
and he will lift you up in honor.

JAMES 4:10

God reveals just enough of the future to increase your dependence on him. God alone knows everything about the future, and he wants you to be a part of his work in it, so you must rely on him to lead you there. That is the essence of what it means to live by faith.

Faith is trusting God to lead you into the future he promises you rather than trying to create your own future by yourself.

Are you charting your own future, or are you following God to the future he has for you?

More Than a Victor

*The Lord is faithful; he will strengthen you
and guard you from the evil one.*

2 THESSALONIANS 3:3

*The Lord will deliver me from every
evil attack and will bring me safely
into his heavenly Kingdom.*

2 TIMOTHY 4:18

You are in the middle of a spiritual battle. As soon as you became a Christian, they began to attack you, trying to conquer your heart and turn you against God. The battle is over your very soul, so you must fight with all your strength and every weapon God gives you.

You cannot defeat Satan while you live on this earth, but Jesus has already won the victory. When you trust him to fight for you, you will be victorious in this life and in eternity.

———— • ————

*Are you losing the battle, or are you expecting
God to give you victory, both now and forever?*

Finishing Strong

*I am certain that God, who began the good work
within you, will continue his work until
it is finally finished on the day
when Christ Jesus returns.*

PHILIPPIANS 1:6

Another year has slipped by, and you wonder where the time went and how it went so quickly. That's why it is so important to do your best each day, whether in your work, your relationships, or your walk with God.

Be faithful to carry out the responsibilities and the call that God will give you in the new year to come. Then at the end of next year, you will have the satisfaction of finishing a job well done and experiencing the pleasure of God.

*Have you finished well this year?
What goals can you set now so that you
will finish well next year too?*

Topical Index